John Hunt was educa.... ... ., and Wadham College, Oxford. His career as an educationalist culminated as Headmaster of the prestigious girls' school Roedean in Sussex. His lifelong interest in historical geography includes research on seventeenth century Dutch-Scottish east coast trade, and writing articles on fine arts, architecture and travel for leading journals.

John Hunt

DUTCH
SOUTH AFRICA

*Early Settlers at the Cape
1652 to 1708*

Edited by
Heather-Ann Campbell

Matador
9 De Montfort Mews
Leicester LE1 7FW, UK
Tel: (+44) 116 255 9311 / 9312
Email: books@troubador.co.uk
Web: www.troubador.co.uk/matador

ISBN 1 904744 95 8

Cover illustration: *Ships in Table Bay* by Aernout Smit, 1683

Typeset in 11pt Palatino by Troubador Publishing Ltd, Leicester, UK
Printed by The Cromwell Press, Trowbridge, Wilts, UK

Matador is an imprint of Troubador Publishing

Contents

Introduction   vii
Acknowledgements   xi
List of Plates   xiii

Chapter 1   Arrival of the Dutch at the Cape   1

Chapter 2   Jan van Riebeeck's initiatives   10

Chapter 3   Van Riebeeck's developing community   24

Chapter 4   Hazards of the sea   41

Chapter 5   Slaves, freemen and burghers   53

Chapter 6   Van Riebeeck's later years   65

Chapter 7   Lean years of weak leadership   79

Chapter 8   Consolidation under two governors   95

Chapter 9   Impact of Simon van der Stel   106

Chapter 10   In search of copper   129

Chapter 11   Arrival of the Huguenots   135

Chapter 12   Years of expansion   142

Chapter 13   Willem Adriaan's misjudgments   159

Chapter 14   Downfall of Willem Adriaan   174

Chapter 15   Collapse of the Dutch East India Company   184

To Sarah, Jonathan and Richard

Introduction

This work is an account of the Dutch settlement at the Cape of Good Hope during its formative years from 1652 to 1708. It was the first European settlement in Africa south of the Sahara. The climate, similar to the Mediterranean with warm wet winters and hot dry summers, encouraged farming. The natural fresh-water spring line from the base of Table Mountain ensured a reliable water supply for domestic use and for the growing of crops.

These advantages were first discovered in 1647 when the *Haarlem*, a Dutch ship returning to the Netherlands from the East Indies, was wrecked on the sands of Table Bay. The crew, who were stranded for nearly a year before being rescued, were greatly impressed by the speed with which edible plants and fruit would grow.

The central theme is the Dutch East India Company, better known by its initials VOC for Vereenigde Oostindische Compagnie, and its pattern of trade in spices between its far eastern headquarters at Batavia and the rich markets of the Netherlands and Europe.

A ruling committee, known as the Council of Seventeen, administered the settlement and the fleets plying to and from the East from its headquarters in Amsterdam, where it kept a tight rein on expenditure for settlement and farming developments at the Cape.

On behalf of the Council of Seventeen, regular visits to the Cape were made by a Commissioner, whose duty it was to advise the current Commander of any perceived shortcomings and necessary remedial action. The reports of the Commissioners are an integral source of information and comment in the VOC records.

The Cape settlement was largely developed as a staging post to provide a supply of fresh food and water for the fleets as they passed on their way to and from the Far East. The influence of the VOC in its administration from Amsterdam was forceful and, at a distance of 6000 miles from the Cape, was surprisingly effective up to 1708 after which time ever increasing debts undermined the Company which collapsed in 1795 and was finally dissolved in 1799.

The source material for this book is largely drawn from the records and diaries of the VOC and its Commanders, which have been translated from the Dutch.★ These comprise a fascinating chronicle of the times written by the successive Commanders of the Cape who varied greatly in their acumen, Simon van der Stel being the most notable. Documents and letters passing between Amsterdam and the Cape give a vivid contemporary account of the growth of the settlement, starting with the site of Cape Town in 1652 and later moving east to Stellenbosch.

Among the first tasks of the early settlers was the building of an earthen fort as a defence against wild animals. This was the first settlement on the shores of Table Bay, with the impressive 2000 foot Table Mountain behind it. The first Dutch Commander at the Cape was Jan van Riebeeck. His detailed journal provides an

---

★Important sources include: G.M.Theal, *Chronicles of the Cape Commanders*, Cape Town,W.A. Richards & Sons, 1882;Van Riebeeck Society, *Journal of Jan van Riebeeck*, translated in 1952, 3 vols.; H.C.V. Leibbrandt, *Précis of the Archives of the Cape of Good Hope*: containing Letters Received and Letters Despatched, 1695–1708, 3 vols., Cape Town,W.A. Richards & Sons, 1896–1900.

intimate record of the problems and disasters that faced the early settlers in their struggle for survival. It vividly portrays the relations between the newly arrived Dutch and the indigenous tribes they encountered and the slow progress towards a more organized community.

Acknowledgements

Special thanks are due to the late Mrs Petronell Jarvis of Cape Town for much help with references and introductions. Petronell Jarvis became an enthusiast for my research based on her strong sense of local history. Grateful thanks go to Philip Erskine of Ida's Valley Homestead, Stellenbosch, for discussions on the first Dutch settlers in South Africa. Thanks go to Dr Pieter Jansen of Middelburg and to Dr John McCracken.

Grateful thanks go to institutions for help and for permission to reproduce material in their possession including the Van Riebeeck Society, Cape Town; The Iziko William Fehr Collection, Cape Town Castle; Rijksmuseum, Amsterdam; The National Maritime Museum, London; Longmans Publishers, London; Cape Archives, Cape Town; Algemeen Rijksarchief, Den Haag; National Library of South Africa, Cape Town; South African Cultural History Museum, Cape Town; Rhodes House Library, Oxford, especially to its former librarian Alan Bell; The Simon van der Stel Foundation, Cape Town; National Botanic Gardens of South Africa, Kirstenbosch; Department of Archaeology, Cape Town University; National Monuments Council, Cape Town; University of Cape Town (especially Dr Ann Markel); Vergelegen Public Relations (especially Mrs Genevieve Faure).

Thanks are also due to the following for enabling the reproduction of maps and illustrations: The Oxford University Press; Van Schaik Publishing Ltd, Pretoria; Barrie & Rockliffe Ltd, London; B.T. Batsford Books Ltd, London; Jonathan Potter Limited, London; Prontaprint, Inverness.

Without the help of my wife Sarah in combing the manuscript and providing assistance in the background, I would have been hard pressed to produce a coherent text.

Most important of all is the tribute due to Mrs Heather-Ann Campbell, without whose enthusiasm and professional expertise this book would not have been published. Her editing skills, untiring patience, humour and imagination have been invaluable.

John Hunt
April 2005

List of Plates

Plate 1
A States Yacht in a fresh breeze running
towards a group of Dutch ships (Painting by
Willem van de Velde the Younger, 1673)

Plate 2
Africae, Guillaume Blaeu, Amsterdam 1619 to c.1650

Plate 3
Insulae Moluccae (Chart from the English edition of
Linschoten's work, London 1598)

Plate 4
Jan van Riebeeck

Plate 5
Maria de la Quellerie, wife of Jan van Riebeeck

Plate 6
Arrival at the Cape of Jan van Riebeeck (Painting by
Charles Bell, 1850)

Plate 7
Cape Colony 1660

Plate 8
R and J Ottens map of Africa

CHAPTER 1

Arrival of the Dutch at the Cape

The seventeenth century was the golden age for the Netherlands and a time of prosperity and enthusiasm. Talented men such as Hals and Rembrandt were renowned painters; mapmakers like Blaeu and Mercator had pioneered work on aids to navigation, used by an increasing number of traders. Craftsmen were building ships at the rate of about 2000 a year to supply the growing needs of the Dutch East India Company, founded in 1602.

Earlier, the Portuguese had been among the first Europeans since classical times to renew on a large scale sea links between Europe and the East. They were among the few European nations in the late fifteenth century with the necessary ship-building and navigational skills and they were strongly motivated to seek new sea routes to gain control of the lucrative maritime spice trade with the Far East. Meanwhile, the Spaniards, competing for navigational trade and power, were more occupied in discovering the New World.

Before the year 1600, it was mainly the Portuguese who had explored sailing routes from northern Europe round the coast of Africa to the Far East. It was Henry the Navigator (1394 to 1460), the great Portuguese pioneer, who had sponsored voyages of discovery down the western coast of Africa which led to the discovery of South Africa as an area for European settlement. He trained a school of pilots and accurate maps and charts were drawn up to facilitate the early Portuguese navigators. These early navigators recorded a number of landfalls and several of the areas they named still bear witness to their nationality. As a landmark at

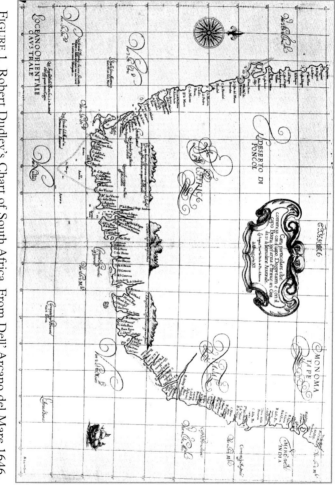

FIGURE 1 Robert Dudley's Chart of South Africa. From Dell' Arcano del Mare 1646.
(Courtesy of B.T. Batsford Ltd)

the junction of the Atlantic and Indian oceans, the Cape had been commented on by generations of explorers starting with the Portuguese Bartolomeu Dias, who, in 1487, discovered the Cape of Good Hope (originally named the 'Cape of Storms') while he was on a voyage from Europe searching for an ocean route to India. The Cape was an intriguing mystery to explorers but no permanent settlement took place until the powerful Dutch East India Company recognised the value of setting up a station on the long route to the Far East, where fresh food and water could be taken on board the Company's fleets when they passed Table Bay twice a year.

A decade later, the great navigator Vasco da Gama was the next contributor to the growing knowledge of ocean routes. He made good use of Dias' recorded knowledge of winds and currents. In less than four months, Vasco da Gama landed just north of the Cape, where he met members of the Khoikhoi community, later to be given the name 'Hottentot' by the Dutch, who hearing a 'click' language thought of their word for a stutterer. Sailing on beyond Dias' furthest point, he reached a new coast on Christmas Day in 1497 which he called Natal. Da Gama completed the voyage to India in the monsoon before returning to Portugal with a cargo of spices so valuable that "it paid the cost of his voyage sixty times over."

Throughout the sixteenth century, the Spanish and Portuguese dominated the trade route via the Cape. However, in spite of their increasing knowledge of the coastline, the Portuguese found no reason to develop or settle in south-west Africa. The territory remained empty of Europeans for another century and a half. A comparison may be drawn here with the settlement of central Chile, which took place after the conquest by the Spanish in 1540 and the founding of Santiago a year later by Valdivia. He praised the 'enchanting climate' and its suitability for agriculture. These factors could equally well be applied to the south-west Cape which, like central Chile, enjoys a Mediterranean type of climate.

Not until the Dutch East India Company took advantage of the
climate, to set up production of garden crops and fruit to sustain
their fleets, did any kind of economic development take place.

The attractions of the Cape climate impressed the Dutch traveller
Joris van Spilbergen. In 1600, he wrote: "As regards the land of
the 'Capa de Buona Esperence', it is very healthy and temperate,
very convenient for cultivation and habitation and for producing
all manner of crops; although it seems to be somewhat mountainous and hilly, it is also adorned with very beautiful side valleys."

As far as is known, the first Englishman to round the Cape was
Thomas Stevens on a voyage to India in 1579, by which time the
route pioneered by the Portuguese was well marked on maps. A
year later, Sir Francis Drake on his voyage round the world made
his celebrated note "this Cape is a most stately thing, and the
fairest Cape we saw in the whole circumference of the earth, and
we passed it on 18 June."

In 1580, Portugal was annexed to Spain and until 1640
Portuguese trade interests were subsumed to Spain. After the
defeat by the English of the Spanish Armada in 1588 and Spain's
failure to subdue the Dutch during the Eighty Years War of
Netherlands independence, the trade route to the East was open
to the English and the Dutch. The Dutch were ahead since they
had larger resources and they went straight to the East Indies, the
main source of spices, especially mace, nutmeg and cloves, to
Ceylon for many spices, especially cinnamon, and to south India
for cardamoms and pepper.

The growth of Dutch trading with the East Indies led to the rapid
expansion of demand for spices. These could be readily sold in
the markets of Europe where interest in spices and other food
enhancements was fast growing. The Spanish king, in 1598, during the union between Spain and Portugal, closed the key port of
Lisbon to the Dutch. This was among the chief reasons for the

great expansion of the Netherlands' independent trade with the East. Before the union, the Dutch had been the main carriers of eastern produce from Lisbon to northern Europe and they were now forced to sail to the East to make up for the loss of the port of Lisbon.

It was because small European trading companies tended to lack the financial backing necessary for large scale operations that the Dutch East India Company was formed in 1602, chartered by the Dutch States General, on a joint-stock basis with investment open to all. It quickly became the most extensive and far-reaching maritime trading company in Europe, outpacing its English rival, the English East India Company, which had been given its charter two years earlier, with an initial capital only one-tenth that of the Dutch company. Until 1612, the English company was organised on a single-voyage basis, financed by groups of merchants within the company. Later it was financed by terminable joint stocks for operations over a number of years and a permanent capital fund was only established in 1657. Between 1613 and 1632, the Dutch drove the English from the Spice Islands and the Malay Archipelago almost entirely.

The Dutch East India Company, commonly known by its Dutch initials the VOC (Vereenigde Oostindische Compagnie) was endowed with political and economic powers second to none. Its critics held it to be an organisation of licensed piracy and international greed but it was certainly spectacular in its operations. When the Netherlands reached a zenith in the seventeenth century, the time was ripe for a trading association on the scale of the VOC. The Company was run by a highly select and autocratic body in Amsterdam known as the Council of Seventeen (the 'Heeren' or Lords XVII). The seventeen directors received a monopoly of navigational rights eastwards around the Cape of Good Hope and westwards through the Straits of Magellan. They were empowered to make treaties with native rulers on behalf of the States-General, set up garrisoned forts and appoint governors and justices. The Council was made up of representatives of each of the main ports or chambers in the Netherlands of which Amsterdam had eight representatives; Zeeland had four; Enkhuizen and Hoorn, and Delft and Rotterdam, had two respectively. The seventeenth member was nominated in succession by the other members of the United Netherlands' independent states. In rotation, each chamber selected one member in turn, except for Amsterdam, and the Lords Seventeen served for a term of office lasting three years. They were a practical group consisting of experienced traders and merchants who met twice a week.

East India House was the administrative headquarters of the Company in Amsterdam. It was here that every ship's captain went before a voyage to collect necessary charts and information. Relatives and friends bade farewell at the Weeping Tower knowing that they would not see their loved ones for at least a year and possibly not at all. The chief departure point was Texel, to which crews were taken by barge because the depth of water in the Zuider Zee was inadequate for a laden ship. At Texel, the ships gathered from all the different chambers and were moored on the seaward side in deep water. Although December or January was the chief departure time, some fleets were able to set out in spring or late summer.

The wealth which trade brought to the Netherlands, especially in the seventeenth century, may be seen today in patronage given to architecture, painting and furniture in many parts of that country. Small historic ports on the former Zuider Zee such as Enkhuizen and Hoorn in particular are shining examples of the great days of Dutch trade overseas, especially in the Far East. The shipping museum at Hoorn has a collection of the spices that were among the main contents of the ships' cargoes. These included white and black pepper, cloves, nutmeg, mace, and cinnamon. Also in the collection are exhibits of tea, rice, cane sugar, saltpeter and soyabean. The historic glitter of Dutch prosperity evident in the

Town Hall in Amsterdam, which was built by van Kampen in 1648, or the spacious merchants' houses on the Herrengracht, derives largely from the wealth of the VOC. The Company initials became almost a trademark on ships' transoms, flags, porcelain and other equipment.

The VOC shipyards were close to Amsterdam on the river Ij. Many types of ships were built there, the East Indiamen and 'Fluyt' ships being the most commonly used for long-haul trade to the East Indies. This Flute, as the English called it, was a small supply vessel rigged as a 'pink' with three masts, and manned by relatively few hands, carried a bulky cargo, mounted few or no guns, and could be built cheaply and in large numbers. Timber for construction came from Germany, where the shipwrights could first go to inspect what was available. Oak logs, floated down the Rhine to the Netherlands, provided the largest source of timber for the shipyards. By the end of the sixteenth century, there was a growing need for marine insurance and, in 1598, Amsterdam organised a chamber of assurance in order to meet the demand. Within seven years of the foundation of the VOC, the Amsterdam Lending Bank was formed in 1609 and the Exchange Bank was formed in 1614 to deal with the ever-increasing trade.

With the expansion of trade between the Netherlands and the East Indies, the Council of Seventeen passed a resolution in the year 1616 that its fleets should call in at Table Bay to rest the crews before rounding the Cape of Good Hope on the second half of the journey. Three years later, the Council debated the idea of setting up a VOC victualling or refreshment station but no further action was taken. The fleet did indeed call at Table Bay from 1616 and the ships recorded their presence by marking stones with the dates of their visits. Letters were placed under these stones and were collected, sometimes months later, by the homeward bound ships and taken to Holland. From the beginning of the seventeenth century, both English and Dutch ships were putting in at the Cape of Good Hope to take on fresh water from the streams which flowed down from Table Mountain. It was this natural asset that was to have a strong influence on the pattern of the settlement when cultivation was eventually started in 1652 by Jan van Riebeeck.

In the early 1600s, it had looked as if the English rather than the Dutch might be the first European settlers in South Africa. The first English East India Company fleet anchored in Table Bay in 1601. By 1614, the Company intended to create a station with ten convicts but the idea came to nothing. In June 1620, two commodores of the English East India Company fleet, Andrew Shillinge and Humphrey Fitzherbert, staked a claim on the Cape with the idea that it should formally become a victualling station for the English fleet. On 3 July 1620, they hoisted the British flag on Table Mountain. When news of this reached England, it was not taken seriously, and the commodores had meanwhile sailed on to the East where Shillinge was reputed to have died in a fight and Fitzherbert from drink. Thus concluded a colourful episode which, had circumstances been otherwise, could have resulted in a very different history of European settlement at the Cape.

Meanwhile, the English East India Company had spread its activities to Indonesia and sharpened its competition with the Dutch. Partly as a result of this challenge, in 1611, the headquarters of Dutch operations moved from the (now in ruins) port of Bantam to the old trading centre Jacatra (Jakarta) near the north coast of Java. In 1619, it was renamed Batavia. This was a poetic name for the Netherlands, derived from the Batavi, an ancient Germanic tribe which inhabited the region around the site of Leiden by the mouth of the Oude Rijn (Old Rhine).

By 1619, increased shipping was plying between the Netherlands and Batavia, which became the commercial headquarters of the VOC in that year. More than twenty years were to elapse before any further developments took place at the Cape. The origin of permanent settlement was the result of an accident to a ship of the

Dutch East India Company, the *Haarlem*, which set sail from Batavia in January 1647. Shipwreck was not uncommon and the voyage of the *Haarlem* ended when she was driven on to the sandy shores of Table Bay in 1647. It was, however, of the greatest importance to future plans for European settlement at the Cape. While the crew of VOC sailors were marooned there for nearly a year, they formed a favourable impression of their surroundings, particularly the climate and fertility of the soil and the friendliness of the reputedly fierce Khoi inhabitants of the Cape. Two of their members, Leendert Jansz, who was captain of the survivors, and Nicholas Proot, compiled a report which briefly set out "the advantage and profit which will accrue to the United Chartered East India Company from making a Fort and Garden at the Cabo de Boa Esperence." Dated 26 July 1649, the document was presented to the Council of Seventeen and it made a strong case for setting up a VOC establishment. "Everything will grow as well as in any other place in the world, particularly pumpkins, watermelons, cabbages, carrots, radishes, turnips, onions, leeks and every other kind of vegetables as we, of the wrecked ship *Haarlem*, have experienced and can testify."

Seldom known for their speed of action, the Seventeen, after a delay of almost two years, sought an opinion on the report from one of their administrative staff who had held a post in the Far East and who had spent three weeks with the *Haarlem*'s survivors at the Cape in 1648. This man was Jan van Riebeeck.

CHAPTER 2

Jan van Riebeeck's Initiatives

Jan van Riebeeck was to play a key role in laying the foundations of Dutch South Africa. He was born on 21 April 1619 of a family whose name dates back to the fourteenth century. His father was a sea captain and his mother was a daughter of Govert Anthoniszoon, Mayor of Culemborg, a small town several miles south-east of Utrecht. Van Riebeeck was only eleven when his mother died at Schiedam. Ten years later, his father died at Pernambuco in Brazil while on business for the Netherlands West India Company. It is probable that van Riebeeck spent much of his childhood at the home of his grandfather the Mayor, whose responsibilities would have given the boy a breadth of education that he would not otherwise have received.

As a young man taking up a career, van Riebeeck prepared himself for medicine through an apprenticeship to a surgeon. He completed his training in 1639, not long before the death of his father. Deciding that he wished to pursue his career in the service of the VOC, he made an application through the Chamber of Delft and in April 1639 he was appointed assistant surgeon. In the same month, he sailed for the East Indies in the *Hof van Holland* in the knowledge that the voyage could take anything between six and nine months.

In July, two months after leaving the Netherlands, the ship was wrecked on the coast of West Africa at Sierra Leone. The shipwreck meant that van Riebeeck's arrival at Batavia was delayed for another year, a full fifteen months after he had started out. Unexpected disillusionment with medicine quickly set in and he was trans-

FIGURE 2 The Castle, Batavia, circa 1656. Painting by A. Beeckman. (Reproduced courtesy of the Rijksmuseum, Amsterdam).

ferred to work involving administration and trade, which he found more exciting than the role of a medical officer. He became assistant at the VOC headquarters in Batavia and proved himself to be quick and intelligent. He went on to Japan and in 1645 took charge of the VOC trading station at Tonkin, before returning to Amsterdam in 1648, in disgrace, accused of private trading.

Having returned to the Netherlands, van Riebeeck met his future wife, Maria de la Quellerie, who was ten years younger than he. Her father had been a minister in Rotterdam and had died when Maria was only a year old. Her grandfather was a French noble-man who later became a Huguenot preacher and had to flee his country in 1572 to avoid the Massacre of St. Bartholomew's Day, going first to England and then to the Netherlands. Van Riebeeck married Maria, who was then twenty one years old, in 1649, and together they set up house in Amsterdam. Although occupied in the city with commerce, van Riebeeck hankered after further employment with the VOC. When the Seventeen asked him to comment on the report of Jansz and Proot, he seized the oppor-tunity to write a favourable critique, which impressed the Seventeen. Subsequently, they appointed him leader of the pro-posed VOC expedition to the Cape.

In March 1651, the Seventeen issued instructions for the Commander and his party, who were to travel in three ships, *Dromedaris, Reijger* and the yacht *Goede Hoop*. After arriving at the Cape, 6000 miles from the Netherlands, they were, according to instructions, "to provide that the passing and re-passing of East India ships, to and from Batavia respectively, may without acci-dent touch at the said Cape or Bay, and also upon arrival there, may find the means of procuring herbs, fresh water, and other needful refreshments and by this means restore the health of their sick. It is necessary that a general rendezvous be formed near the shore of the said Cape." Among the other detailed requirements of the Council of Seventeen was the construction of a small for-tified trading station to be named the 'Goede Hoop'. In the fort, there was to be accommodation for seventy to eighty persons and, as soon as it was ready, attention was to be given to the establishment of gardens "taking for this purpose all the best and richest ground". It would also be necessary to "make inspection near the fort for the land best suited for de-pasturing and breeding cattle, for which purpose a good correspondence and intelligence with the natives will be very necessary, in order to reconcile them in time to your customs, above all, taking care that you do not injure them in person."

After several months of preparation and delay, the party sailed for South Africa from Texel on Christmas Eve 1651. Van Riebeeck was accompanied by his wife, their infant son Lambertus and two nieces to whom he was guardian, Elizabeth and Sebastiana van Opdorp. Maria van Riebeeck was the first of a large number of competent women to go to the Cape; she was attractive both in appearance and manner and a great support to her husband. During their years at the Cape, a visitor said of Maria, "she is indisputably one of the most perfect women that I have seen and everybody likes her."

Approached from the sea, the full majesty of the setting of Table Bay against its backdrop of Table Mountain would have made a strong impact. It would have been a welcome sight to those who had suffered the rigours of life on a sailing ship. Van Riebeeck's party arrived on 6 April 1652 after a journey which had taken three and a half months. Arriving towards autumn, the group was fortunate to have a few months of good weather before the blustery winter storms of the south-east trade winds set in. However, the new arrivals must have viewed the site of what was to be their new encampment with some trepidation and dismay. The land would have been wild and bleak, inhabited by hippopotamuses, lions, snakes, ostriches, monkeys, elephants, and other strange animals, the trees tall and sparse, and the dominating Table Mountain possibly shrouded in that peculiar mist later to become known as the Devil's Tablecloth. From the three ships, van

FIGURE 3 Khoisan in strong south-easter.
(Reproduced by permission of the National Library of South Africa)

Riebeeck sent ashore one hundred men to work and left eighty one on board to mind the ships and bring ashore the construction materials and tools, including "shovels, spades, picks, mattocks and wheelbarrows."

The list just quoted comes from the detailed journal which van Riebeeck kept during his years at the Cape. This extract and many to follow come from his meticulous record of the activities and development of the VOC settlement. The journal noted that when they started to build the fort, it was often difficult to make secure walls from such loose soil as they found and the use of small branches helped to bind the construction together, although it was not exactly wattle and daub. It was feared that heavy rain might wash away the construction altogether.

A note of anxiety at times crept into the diary: "We are also putting the men to work properly, for there are very few among them who understand the job." Van Riebeeck was to find the task of maintaining a garrison and a manual workforce from so small a number difficult. Some three weeks after their arrival at Table Bay, another entry in the diary focused on this problem. "The gardener sent with us from the Fatherland is busy on a few plots of ground, sowing some seeds by way of experiment; but little as yet can be achieved in this respect as the men are too much needed for the work on the fortification."

The European settlers were to meet two groups of indigenous peoples, the San or 'Bushmen', and the Khoikhoi or 'Hottentots' as the Dutch named them. The San, diminutive, fleet-footed nomads, were always on the move with their lifestyle dependent on hunting and gathering foods. They tended to live in the more mountainous regions east of the Cape lowlands, where they had little impact on the Dutch and vice versa. The Khoi were short of stature, with yellowish-brown skin and reared their cattle on the better quality grasslands of the Cape lowlands. They were sometimes in conflict with the Dutch settlers, who grazed the same areas of land but needed to trade with the Khoi for their meat supply. This custom was of benefit to both sides and recurred throughout the years of the VOC at the Cape. Around Table Bay, the Goringhaikona tribe lived on seafood from along the coast and had no herds.

The need of the settlers to secure a good supply of local food was a constant problem. Soon after their arrival, a small party was dispatched a short distance to the east on a fishing excursion near the Salt River. They returned cheerfully with "a catch of about seven hundred and fifty lovely steenbrass, including four other delicate fish more tasty than any fish in the Fatherland could be." They also gathered wild sorrel and mustard leaves. The fishing party met a small group of Khoi who were rearing cattle in the area and who "adopted such an amicable and pleasant attitude that it was almost a wonder." The Khoi indicated that copper and tobacco would be a means of bartering cattle. The first bargain of this kind was struck at the end of the new settlers' first week when three small copper plates and three pieces of copper wire were exchanged for a cow and a young calf. This welcome meat was eaten next day for Sunday lunch accompanied by home-grown vegetables.

Clearly there was an expert butcher among the new arrivals, although no reference was ever made to him. Enthused with the success of the first fishing party, they soon arranged another at Salt River. This party landed a catch mainly of steenbrass "in number between nine hundred and a thousand." Not many days later their skills were challenged when a hippopotamus was caught, "the weight of two ordinary fat oxen," which proved very good to eat. An early Sunday excursion inland towards Table Mountain revealed "wide and level ground consisting of exceedingly fine garden soil and clay lands." On the further side of Table Mountain, van Riebeeck was impressed by a landscape which appeared flat and fertile stretching southwards towards False Bay, the southern inlet of the Cape Peninsula. Part of this area was later to become the southern suburbs of Cape Town from Rondebosch to Muizenberg.

By 15 May 1652, the fort was sufficiently far advanced "to be named Goede Hoop in accordance with the instruction of our Lords and Masters," and van Riebeeck's journal noted that they named the bastions or points after the ships then lying at anchor, namely: the south point *Dromedaris*, the east point *Walvis*, the west point *Oliphant*, and the north point *Reijger*. Later in the month, the arrival of the *Hof van Zeelandt* from Holland brought news of the appalling conditions during the voyage which was typical of so many. There had been thirty seven deaths and two others had jumped overboard in desperation, but the remaining men were mostly well and healthy.

The first Cape winter for the early settlers was not an enjoyable experience. Attributing illness to changeable weather and scanty accommodation, van Riebeeck recorded in his journal that many were laid low with "the bloody flux as well as other diseases and fevers." The flux carried off the chief carpenter, Hendrik Janssen of Utrecht, a craftsman who could ill be spared. Early in June, the journal recorded: "with planks and old tarred canvas we cannot keep our bread and other dry goods properly dry." In an attempt to improve this shortcoming, there was much culling of rushes or reeds for thatched dwellings, found behind the spur of high ground later to be known as the Lion's Rump. Eager to explore the surrounding area whenever he could, van Riebeeck investigated the hinterland of Table Mountain. At a distance of six miles, he found a vast forest of large, tall, straight, heavy and medium trees suitable for construction work, but he went on to comment on the difficulties of hauling the timber: "The trees are, however, so far away and difficult to convey that it would be less expensive to buy wood in Holland or Batavia and have it sent here than to have it brought from the forest."

Among the many domestic worries, the need for good thatchers was all too apparent because the thatch that had already been laid was so untidy that it would have to be taken down and started all over again. Meanwhile, they were living in very leaky tents. Efforts to procure a consistent supply of meat were often hazardous. "It is often the case that we catch more fish than we require. It is to be wished that cattle, sheep and other livestock were obtainable in equal abundance for feeding and refreshing those who are lying sick, and the hardworking labourers, who have had to content themselves with stale food and sometimes a little fish, and to do their heavy work on this." Some progress was, however, made in early October when a discussion took place with a party of Khoi about barter for cattle. In addition to copper and tobacco, which had already been successfully used, the Khoi enquired about bread because they had tasted 'bread' or ship's biscuit from some English ships "whole bags full of bread and much tobacco and cans full of arrack and wine." Embarrassed by this revelation, the Dutch felt that they should be better provided in order to outdo the English and become the more popular with the natives, if they wished to draw them from the interior. Otherwise, they feared there would not be a single animal to be procured.

Comments on the physical hardships were frequently a source of concern in the journal. Lying in the trade wind belt, much damage was caused by the force of the Cape south-easter winds. "We had quite an ado to keep our dwellings standing by propping them up with supports and the tarred tents were torn into rags." The wind did harm to crops that were growing in exposed sites: "the wheat was blown flat on the ground and almost all the Roman beans and many of the green pea plants, already full of peas and blossoms, were also flattened." But the diary could portray a more optimistic side. A farewell dinner was given by van Riebeeck for ships' officers about to depart to sea and he proudly recorded that everything on the table was produced at the Cape, including the fowls, new green peas, spinach, chervil, pot-herbs, asparagus "a finger's thickness" and lettuce as hard as cabbage and weighing at least one and a quarter pounds each.

There was a good deal of experiment in the early gardening, both with regard to the soil variety and to the local climate. Turnips, for example, proved troublesome in the rich soil close behind the fort, but it was found that all crops apparently did better once the soil had been allowed to settle longer after being dug up five or six times and prepared with manure from the cattle.

Trading contacts with the Khoi from further north became increasingly frequent but remained erratic. Problems arose when cattle now in the possession of the VOC were "released" during the night. A key figure in the barter trade was a young Khoi named Harry, who had an influence which the Commander distrusted. Harry spoke broken English and claimed, according to the diary, to have induced the Saldanhars, a tribe from the coast further north, to start negotiating with them but they regarded him with suspicion, the more so as he had proposed that for every beast obtained by barter he should receive a one-pound copper plate. To this he pretended to have a claim as brokerage. For a number of years, Harry was to give the European settlers, with their fragile existence, an uneasy time in their vital quest for supplies of meat.

The fierce south-easter featured again in November 1652, when many of the crops standing high above the ground, such as peas, beans, barley and wheat, had been blown to the ground by the strong wind and totally ruined. The plot near the fort was more successful and pumpkins growing there were "coming up beautifully and luxuriantly." However, before the end of the year, there was an acute food shortage made worse by an inability to catch fish owing to the worn out state of the nets. After seven months of intensive building works, other equipment too showed signs of wear and tear with the many shovels and spades being broken and wheelbarrows getting very worn. At the same time, there were twenty four people in the hospital suffering from aching joints, blamed on stale food and intense labour.

Shortly after Christmas 1652, however, the first butter was

churned and experiments with cheese-making were made. There was a supply of eggs for the sick, with the fowls breeding satisfactorily. But the pigs and pigeons did not seem to thrive so well. The pigs had not produced any young, and the pigeons had not increased by more than seven, to a total of only fifteen. Meanwhile, the supply of milk and churned butter became increasingly successful, and they could look forward to baking bread from new wheat.

The discipline of van Riebeeck's growing community was not always good. A provost marshal had to be appointed to improve matters because "many of our men do not scruple to sleep on guard duty during the night and commit great thefts from the Company's goods and implements, as well as from the young and mature crops in the gardens." The new appointment was not an instant success because the carpenter's shop was broken into two days later and some of its contents stolen, including the carpenter's clothes in which the thief then dressed himself and paraded around the community.

A note of increasing confidence was recorded when the revictualling of ships was considered. From April to October, the best refreshment of all kinds of pot-herbs and fresh garden produce such as lettuces, beetroots and chervil were available; and for ships that came in February and March there would usually be cattle, carrots and turnips, with milk available throughout the year. With the juxtaposition of cattle and carrots one may conjure up a vivid and rather quaint picture of the loading of cargo.

Early in the New Year of 1653, the diary noted the inconvenience caused to works by the summer south-easters: "No wheelbarrows could be pushed along the planks (on the fort) on account of the strong wind and it was hard enough to walk empty-handed and remain standing. And as a result of the dry wind, the earth is becoming hard and as difficult to dig up as hard rock." Not long after, van Riebeeck expressed one of his understandable bouts of irritation with some of his community when over-indulgence in eating wild figs led to dysentery after the men had "feasted so excessively." It annoyed him that the men were so indifferent about their health and knew no moderation before they had to take to their beds. On a brighter note "the cabbages are growing extraordinarily well; fine heads and are thriving as well as in the Fatherland, likewise the carrots and turnips, with which according to every sign we shall be reasonably well supplied by the arrival of the return fleet. These together with the bartered cattle will serve as excellent refreshment for the ships."

A week later, wheat threshing began for the first time but "it is a pity the south-east wind is so violent here, otherwise enough of all sorts of grain and fruits could be cultivated."

Van Riebeeck believed there would be less exposure to wind damage in the valley beyond the Salt River and that land could accordingly be cultivated with advantage by freemen. These were original VOC employees who had served five years in the Company and who then became independent traders. Van Riebeeck went on to report that the land "is rich, fine and level, with many exceedingly fine fresh rivers running through it." Ever concerned about difficulties regarding food supply, van Riebeeck wrote of the possibility at some future date of salting oxen in barrels in the cold season to the advantage of the Company. He was impressed by the prospect of eight to ten miles of good well-drained land adjoining Table Mountain, which could be used for the rearing of cattle and sheep. Annoyed by what he suspected was a loss of cattle through the inattention of the herdsmen, he had the cattle counted. He complained: "Where there should have been one hundred and thirty eight head, only one hundred and twenty six could be accounted for, the others had disappeared through the carelessness of the guards as stated before."

A widening of activities designed to help improve the trading opportunities of the VOC included the hunting of seals for their skins. Fifteen hundred dried sealskins were brought down from Saldanha Bay. A sharp criticism of the men involved was evident in the journal's comment that twice as many skins could have been obtained if the hunters had been better equipped and if they had been allowed to share in the proceeds rather than being on a fixed low wage.

On 18 January 1653, there was a welcome diversion with the arrival of the galiot *Swarte Vos*, a small cargo vessel, with everyone on board said to be in good health. The ship, which had come to the Cape via Brazil, had sailed from Texel in the Netherlands four months previously and it brought the serious news of a naval war between England and the Netherlands. This was the first of the three Anglo-Dutch Wars, the naval conflicts fought between England and the newly independent United Provinces of the Netherlands from 1652 to 1674. In 1672, the Dutch were fighting the third war with the English, who were sometimes allied to the French as part of the Great War of Louis XIV which involved most of Europe until 1678. An immediate cause of the naval skirmishes was the two nations' commercial rivalry to gain possession of the seas and trade routes, especially in the race to the fabled Spice Islands.

The *Swarte Vos* carried secret orders for the commanders and officers of the return fleet. The vulnerability of the fort and its defences was now a priority and work on the fort was to be redoubled with all available help until it was complete. The journal recorded: "With the fort as it is we are still rather exposed to attack, particularly with regard to defence in European wars." A little bribery was offered in the form of an extra month's salary to the men if they made faster progress with the work. Meanwhile, the galiot was sent across the bay to Robben Island to try to procure and augment supplies and to salt some penguins and young seals for feeding the men on land. It was further noted that supplies would last only another two weeks and the bread supply for only a month.

The galiot *Swarte Vos* also made a journey to Dassen Island, further north than Robben Island, and returned with one hundred live rock rabbits and a cask full of salted ones. Plenty of seals and whales had been seen at Dassen Island but van Riebeeck remained uncertain as to the likely success of establishing a trade link to obtain these resources. He was concerned about the views of the Council of Seventeen and would not have expected it to encourage a financially risky operation since its administration was well known to be tight-fisted.

The fort might have been vulnerable to attack from fighting men but at least it proved a safe haven against intruding animals. One night lions created a disturbance by roaring when they scented sheep which had been safely enclosed in the fort, as if they wanted to tear everything to pieces, but to no avail since the surrounding walls were fortunately too high for them to scale.

CHAPTER 3

Van Riebeeck's Developing Community

The chief means of communication between the Council of Seventeen and the infant Cape community was vested in the Council of Policy. This organisation spanned the entire length of Dutch rule at the Cape from 1652 to 1795 and it was responsible for administering the policies of the VOC. Minutes were kept of all its meetings and records of its resolutions were passed to Amsterdam and Batavia under the heading of 'Letters Despatched.' Incoming orders from the Seventeen were recorded as 'Letters Received.' It could take up to a year for answers to be received at the Cape but the system worked.

In its earliest form the Council of Policy consisted of only four members: the Commander of the Cape and three skippers. After four years, the membership was changed to a more permanent team consisting of the Commander, the sergeant and the book-keeper. When there was a fleet in Table Bay, its chief officers joined the Council in an enlarged body known as the Broad Council. The chairman of this enlarged committee was the most senior individual present, either the Cape Commander or one of the visiting officers.

At first the Council had three functions: legislation, administration and justice. All the official dispatches received by the Council had to be opened by the chairman in the presence of the Council and read out to them. Among its earliest detailed functions were the making of laws for the better administration of the Cape, levying taxation, the granting of land in freehold or on lease, and appointing VOC employees to civil occupations. The secretary to the Council kept minutes of all meetings which were then signed by those who had been present at the meeting.

The Council was kept busy to judge by the amount of paperwork which it generated. From 1656 onwards, its judicial work was taken over by the newly founded Court of Justice. A classic example of the background to a Broad Council meeting occurred on 2nd March 1653 with the arrival of the outward-bound fleet consisting of five ships under the charge of Admiral Demmer who had been Governor of Amboina from 1642 to 1647. The ships were the *Hof van Zeelandt, Walvis, Parel, Princess Roijael,* and *Molucca.* The Admiral was pleased to see the fortifications and he presided at a meeting of the Broad Council. Van Riebeeck suggested that a loan of two hundred men for a period of two weeks would enable the completion of the fort but the Council did not agree. Van Riebeeck told the Council "our men are fatigued, worn out and starved as a result of the continual labour and scanty victuals." The fleet was, however, prepared to land food from each ship to the quantity of a last (about 80 bushels) of rice, one barrel of meat and some bread. For restocking the ship, each vessel was to receive "three head of cattle and cabbage to go with it" for the crew. For the officers of each ship, there would be a supply of "four sheep as well as cabbage, carrots, beetroot, salad, etc." The Admiral's cabin was to receive six sheep and the Vice-Admiral's five.

On 28 March 1653, the yacht *Haes* arrived from Holland having sailed from Texel six months previously and called at Sierra Leone en route. Admiral Demmer held another Broad Council meeting and decided that the yacht should go on to Batavia as soon as possible after unloading cargo for the Cape. The opportunity was taken to send a report on affairs at the Cape to the Governor-General and Council of India, the chief committee of the administration. Travelling in the other direction, Admiral Demmer and his fleet sailed for Holland before daylight on

17 April 1653 on the south-east wind which would carry them straight out of Table Bay. Next day the yachts *Haes* and *Windhout* sailed for Batavia.

On 18 April the same year, the *Muijden* arrived from Texel without stopping en route and had made the voyage in less than four months, having sailed on 26 December. The crew were "fairly well and only six or seven deaths." Next day, van Riebeeck supplied the yacht with stores consisting of one head of cattle, with cabbages and carrots for the crew and officers. While doing so, the homeward bound ship *Oliphant* arrived from India, having left Batavia on 2 February, a journey of two and a half months. Three days later, the return ship *Provintia* arrived and anchored off Table Bay on 22 April. It was decided that a cargo of 'bread' or biscuit which had been brought to the Cape by the *Muijden*, no doubt rather stale after four months at sea, was to be used instead for the victualling of the return fleet. At the Cape, the storage facilities for six thousand pounds of 'bread' were not adequate and it was felt that better use could be made of rice as an alternative to grain so that the *Oliphant* and *Provintia* were each to take on three thousand pounds of 'bread'.

The need for more lasting building materials led to the use of lime and the making of bricks. The galiot *Swarte Vos* had been dispatched to Robben Island and returned with shells gathered from the shore for lime-burning. Later in the year, another vessel was sent to Robben Island to gather more shells for the limekiln. When they lit the fire in the first limekiln, which was nine fathoms in circumference, it proved to be fairly successful. On 24 March, the brick kiln was completed and the first bricks made. Suitable clay had been found close to the fort. It was the intention to make all the buildings in the fort of bricks so as to be fireproof and "so strong that they would not have to be looked after all the time."

Van Riebeeck's journal dwells from time to time on the importance which he attached to his Christian faith and the strength which he derived from it. There was recognition "of our safe arrival at this place through the Holy guidance of God to build this fortress and establish this settlement according to the instructions of our Lords and Masters, and the Lord God has hitherto given his abundant blessing to the satisfactory and successful accomplishment of all these matters." It is obvious from the journal that one of the Commander's abiding objections was that the Khoi were not Christians. From such sentiments, it is not difficult to see the importance that was attached in later generations of European settlers to their missionary zeal, misplaced though some of it was.

The prospects of good relationships with the Khoi arose from a visitation by them just after the second anniversary of the settlers' arrival. A group of Khoi were seen about one and a half miles from the fort, complete with flocks of sheep and herds of cattle. The settlers saw an entire camp of natives, with women and children, about one hundred strong. The camp consisted of sixteen huts in a circle enclosed by a brushwood surround with two openings for the cattle to go in and out in the morning and evening. The journal reports that when the Dutch approached, they "found the passage very well guarded by about thirty sturdy fellows, their hides and cloaks discarded and quite naked, without the slightest encumbrances in the world, and well provided with weapons, including assegais, bows and arrows. Most of them were the same rogues who had stolen our cattle." Among the herd were at least three which they recognized without any doubt owing to the marks they had made on them.

Van Riebeeck and his companions made a friendly approach: "whereupon a few whom we knew immediately approached us, whereafter we embraced each other like the greatest friends in the world, so that another coat of ours was spoilt as a result of the greasiness of the train-oil and filth with which they and in particular the greatest among them had so besmeared themselves. They shone like looking-glasses in the sun, the fat trickling down from their heads and along their entire bodies, this appearing to be their greatest adornment." The Khoi immediately offered to barter sheep and cattle for copper and tobacco as before, and denied that they were guilty of stealing the settlers' cattle. Van Riebeeck noted that Harry's wife and children were among the group and the visitors were offered drinks of wine all round, to the men, women and children, who in return offered milk and honey and showed them ripe, bitter almonds growing nearby in the forest, said to be good for pigs. On the following day, Verburgh, the book-keeper, and a party of ten or twelve muske-teers went to trade with their friends of the previous day, equipped with copper, tobacco and pipes, but they were given a hostile reception. "The sick-comforter (pastoral helper) received a hard thump on the chest and the book-keeper Verburgh a lusty clout on the head." Van Riebeeck's journal goes on recording that nothing was to be gained by being kind to this faithless crowd. In van Riebeeck's view, a fair revenge should be taken for the "Christian blood" wilfully shed by them.

By the end of March 1653, there was much coming and going of ships of the VOC fleets and an annual pattern had begun to be established. Van Riebeeck and his men could begin to judge the likely demand for food supplies, especially the garden and orchard produce. Its curative vitamin C content was an important antidote to the scurvy engendered by the long voyages, with lim-ited ships' diets taking its toll of the crews. The establishment of the Company's gardens, so named to the present day, forming a prominent part of the centre of Cape Town, took place as antici-pated in that first report of the shipwrecked sailors of the *Haarlem* in 1647.

The Company's gardens soon became a vital part of the life of the settlement on the shores of Table Bay. Their development occu-pied a good deal of the Commander's time and interest. The run-ning of the gardens was delegated to the head gardener, Hendrik Boom, who with his wife and children had travelled out on the

Dromedaris with the van Riebeecks. Annetje Boom, his wife, became a pioneer woman farmer with particular responsibility for looking after milch cows. Eighteen months after the arrival of the Dutch settlers, the Cape community was busy with all the men energetically preparing the gardens in order to have a good supply of produce on hand for the return fleet "there being enough at present in the old garden for the outward bound ships." The old garden was the area around the fort.

After five years as the VOC master gardener, Hendrik Boom was among the first VOC employees who were released from their contracts to become "free burghers" in 1657. While not abandoning his garden interests, Boom was able to devote more time and space to farming. By the end of 1658, the journal records that he owned 40 morgen (about 84 acres), an old bull, ten oxen, eleven cows, two heifers, seven calves, six Dutch and thirty seven Cape sheep, and twenty three pigs. In June 1659, a group of Khoi robbed Boom of his stock and in October Boom's house was burnt to the ground because of the "careless heating of an oven." Later the Boom family returned to Holland, setting a pattern to be followed by others who found the harsh conditions too difficult.

The next master gardener was Marten Jacobs, from Amsterdam. His contribution to the gardens was more of a quiet continuity than a spectacular development; he was in charge from 1657 for about three years before he became a freeman. Van Riebeeck was more enthusiastic about Jacobs' successor, Jacob Huybrehtsen van Roosendael, who had arrived at the Cape in April 1660 from Leiden. A prominent botanist, van Roosendael died prematurely in March 1662, within a year of his appointment, leaving a widow and a young family. In place of van Roosendael, Harman Gresnich was promoted master gardener. He had been at the Cape since 1656, where he had been responsible for the VOC orchards and other plantations behind Table Mountain. Van Riebeeck's journal for 15 April 1662 indicated that Gresnich had been in charge of the Company's gardens since the death of van Roosendael. Gresnich had originally been a nurseryman from Utrecht, and he was the last of the master gardeners to be appointed by van Riebeeck.

Other gardens established by van Riebeeck were in two main areas, both of which lay in the more sheltered land behind Table Mountain. One area covered Rondebosch and Newlands, which were partly used for grain crops. The other area, somewhat higher in altitude, was Boscheuvel, where van Riebeeck established his experimental fruit garden and orchards. It was also the site where he introduced the first vines, an important milestone in the development of the region.

The gardens as seen today in the centre of Cape Town, less extensive than they were in the seventeenth century, are a national monument. Their main axis, however, has continued the direct line from the historic waterfront of Table Bay towards the lower slopes of Table Mountain. This route began as the Herrengracht, now Adderley Street. On this axis, the grid-plan layout of Cape Town was gradually developed and the site of the gardens played a large part in the shaping of it.

In the gardens were grown a wide variety of vegetables and fruit; irrigation in the dry season was provided as needed by the use of streams emerging as springs from the base of Table Mountain. Van Riebeeck himself made careful notes as to the seasonal planting of garden crops. A letter to the Council of Seventeen observed that carrots, parsnips and beet must be in the ground at the latest by the middle of August, followed by the planting and pruning of vines and other trees. About the middle of September, a start would be made on planting watermelon, cucumber and other kinds of melon seeds. In October, cabbages were put into the ground. This could be done the whole year through, but this month was the best in order to have an abundance of vegetables ready when the return squadron and most of the outward bound ships arrived.

Apart from the gardens, the growing of arable crops, especially wheat, was an early experiment in different locations. The first farm was set up at Green Point. Supposedly sheltered by the high ground of the Lion's Rump just to the south, the farm was nevertheless struck by the south-east winds late in the growing season and there were a number of records of the grain being flattened. The second farm was located behind Table Mountain, in a much more sheltered area, at Wynberg, now Bishop's Court, where the crop was much more successful.

Van Riebeeck was a prolific writer both in his journal and in reports sent to the Council of Seventeen in Amsterdam, which he kept closely informed of events at the Cape. Reports and instructions went back and forth between the Cape and Amsterdam and Batavia where the Governor General of Netherlands East India made his headquarters.

Periodically, a senior officer of the VOC would visit the Cape settlement as Commissioner. It was the task of the Commissioner not only to be able to report back in person to the Council of Seventeen but also to issue his own new commands to the Cape authorities if he felt that laws and customs needed to be altered.

The first Commissioner to visit the Cape during van Riebeeck's leadership was Ryklof van Goens, who later in his career became Governor General of the Netherlands East India. His arrival on 17 March 1657 was well timed to investigate the conditions of the newly created "free burghers". These men had been employees of the VOC during the first five years of the settlement and were now applying for a grant of land each with the intention of making themselves independent farmers. Fairly tough conditions were laid on those who aspired to become freemen. Having been granted plots of land of thirteen and a half morgen, about twenty odd acres, free of taxes, for twelve years, they were to concentrate primarily on the growing of grain and were not to be side-tracked into growing tobacco. Nor were they to produce more vegetables than they themselves could consume.

In the interests of increasing the breeding of cattle, they would be allowed to purchase stock from the Khoi but at no higher price than would be paid by the VOC. To protect the cattle from attack by carnivorous beasts, lions, hyenas and leopards might be destroyed and payment would be made at the rate of twenty five guilders, twenty guilders and ten guilders respectively. The farmers had to be of Dutch or German birth, married and of good character and had to undertake to remain for twenty years in South Africa.

Commissioner van Goens had particular responsibility for the conditions of the free burghers. He ordered van Riebeeck to help them to succeed as freemen so that the VOC could save on their wages. The Council of Seventeen were tight-fisted over financial help for the Cape settlement and they insisted that everything be run as economically as possible. In their view, there was no question of spending money freely to improve conditions at the Cape nor of regarding the settlement as anything more than a basic revictualling centre. From an employment point of view, most VOC employees regarded the Cape as a dead end, although there were exceptions to this, as will be seen later.

Van Goens, in his investigation into the activity of the Cape inhabitants, made the suggestion that a canal be constructed to join Table Bay with False Bay. However, this interesting idea was turned down by the Commander on practical grounds. Apart from labour problems, the cost would be too great and maintenance difficulties would be numerous. Although the canal never took shape on the ground, it did appear on a contemporary map of the Cape.

During the year following Commissioner van Goen's visit, a number of others applied to become free burghers in addition to the farmers, including Hendrik Boom, the head gardener. His

FIGURE 4 The Cape and its Vicinity c. 1659. Drawn up in the mid-sixteen hundreds and reproduced by Nieuhof and others. Depicts Van Riebeeck's fort, aborigines and some typical animals: ostriches, snakes, elephants, and lions. Shows some of the freeburghers farms and the canal proposed by visiting Commissioner van Goens in 1655. (*South Africa Panorama*, 1960)

enterprising wife Annetje supplied the VOC market with milk from her cows and also kept a tavern because her husband's wages were insufficient to keep the family. Of the others who sought free burgher status, nine more were farmers, and seven applied as helpers to the new farmers, including an Englishman, Thomas Robinson. Two other Dutchmen, Christian Janssen and Peter Cornellissen, were to be hunters with permission to sell their game and Leendert Cornellissen, who was a ship's carpenter, was granted a strip of forest below Table Mountain and had permission to sell timber. Of the other applicants, two were to set up as tailors, and one as a wagon-maker with access to a strip of forest for his use. There were to be three fishermen and three more were to be sawyers of yellow wood planks for construction work, while the fort surgeon, Jan Vetteman, would be given a wider monopoly to sell his timber. Wouter Mostert, a real pillar of embryonic Cape society for many years to come, had been a miller in Holland and he was given permission to build a new water-operated corn mill, which was the only one of its kind.

Improvements in farming of grain crops led to the urgent need of a proper grain store. For this purpose, a large barn, Groot Schur, was built near the Company's farm at Rondebosch. The barn was a sizeable structure measuring 108 feet by 40 feet. Two years later, it needed to be strengthened by the addition of a thief-proof compound to secure the cattle.

The same year, 1657, saw the construction of a primitive light-house on Robben Island whose fire would be lit when VOC ships were setting sail from Table Bay. From time to time, there were complaints about the shortcomings of this light as a possible safety hazard.

At this time, the European population at the Cape settlement consisted of one hundred and thirty four individuals, Company servants and burghers, men, women and children. There were also at the Cape three male and eight female slaves. A year later, it was noted, in connection with a defence of corn lands against attack by the Khoi that "there were then only ninety seven European men, all told, resident at the Cape, and twenty of these were invalids who had been left behind by the last fleet." It was a hard life which took its toll. There is no doubt that the demands made on the inhabitants by the pressure of the growing economy at the Cape, including the constant need for food supplies, were considerable, not least the threat of disease.

After years of hard work, the construction of the fort was nearing completion. It had been hoped that by 1658 all the brickwork would have been completed for the dwellings, store houses and guard houses within the fort. However, setbacks continued, as illustrated by a colourful incident noted in van Riebeeck's diary, "a leopard broke into the fowl house, killing three of the five geese inside, before going on to attack and bite the sick-comforter in the arm. The cattle, watching the event, stood round in a crescent with lowered horns and the leopard escaped without causing further bloodshed."

In the emerging economy of the Cape settlement, shipbuilding had been among the accomplishments of the Cape craftsmen since 1655. In September of that year, the sloop *Robbejacht* had been launched. It was the second boat to be built; it proved to be useful as a coastal trader running between Table Bay, Robben Island, Dassen Island and Saldanha Bay. Van Riebeeck made his first voyage in the sloop to visit Robben Island, now well-established as part of the VOC administration, to discuss the making of cheese from sheep's milk, since sheep were thriving well there. An old whey expert was taken along to give advice. He suggested using half sheeps' milk and half cows' milk because the cheese would become too rich if sheeps' milk were to be used on its own.

The development of an economy for Robben Island went in fits and starts. It was useful not only for shells for lime burning and later for the rearing of sheep and the culling of penguins, but also to supply penguin, boiled and mixed with vegetable scraps and the green foliage of carrots and turnips to be used as food for pigs. Intermittent correspondence between Jan Wouterssen on Robben Island and the Commander showed how pasture and garden produce was on the increase. Jan Wouterssen wrote somewhat obsequiously "all would be well in the garden if only we had seeds to sow. The cabbage plants are growing well, likewise the carrots. Would your Honour please send us some seeds at the first opportunity. We are sending your Honour 49 goose eggs. A few fowls would also be very useful for hatching out young geese; and a hand barrow or two to carry manure. Lastly, we, your Honour's servants, wish Your Honour a thousand times good night."

A subsequent letter, illustrating the islanders' hardship, read: "We beg Your Honour earnestly and humbly to send us rice instead of barley for our rations as it goes further when eaten with penguin meat. We also ask for a cock and two or three hens which we wish to keep here, then the place will look like a country village." However, Jan Wouterssen was found not to be trusted and in due course was in disgrace for his bad behaviour, "guilty of drunkenness whenever he is able to obtain liquor", and also for neglecting the important task of maintaining the beacon fire as a warning to shipping at night. Thoroughly annoyed by Wouterssen's unreliable behaviour, the Commander arranged to have him and his wife and child dispatched to India at the first opportunity. The assistant on Robben Island, Rijk Overhagen, took over as chief and he quickly showed a better grasp of affairs than had his predecessor.

Still in the busy year of 1657, other events occurred, some of which were to have a lasting influence on life at the Cape. A severe storm in which hailstones as big as pigeons' eggs fell reminded van Riebeeck of earthquakes in India and he expressed devout thanks that they were not experienced at the Cape. During his visit, Commissioner van Goens had given permission for a lodging house to be set up "for the convenience of the men from passing ships." Part of an old sheepfold north of the fort was developed at the expense of the Company to form somewhat austere accommodation. It was to be run by Sergeant van Hawarden whose wife was to keep pigs. An altogether more important structure to be built in the same year, 1657, was the country retreat for the Commander at Rustenburg, later Rondebosch. This house was among the first important buildings to be made of the new locally produced bricks and it was adjacent to an extensive well-planned garden in which the Commander took a close interest. The house was also used as a guest house for distinguished visitors.

As the settlement continued to expand, the ever pressing need to obtain cattle led to the organisation of an adventurous expedition to the interior, expected to last a few weeks. Fifteen Dutchmen were accompanied by four Khoi who were known to them and who would help in the search for the Saldanhars and their cattle. The expedition took nine draught oxen with them. In his diary, the Commander noted that the absence of the men detailed for the expedition and also those assigned for a voyage of the *Robbejacht* at the same time to Saldanha Bay, to fetch a cargo of birds for salting as food, led to a sense of vulnerability at the settlement. "We find our numbers rather few to keep everything going." The expedition set out with considerable quantities of goods to use in the barter trade. The load carried by the oxen was carefully recorded and included 524 pounds weight of copper plate and wire, 48 pounds of tobacco, and one and a half gross of pipes and provisions.

The purpose of the expedition was to discover whether trade with the Saldanhars could be set up direct and without the need to use Harry the Khoi and his accomplices as go-betweens. The intention was to invite the Saldanhars to the fort but there was also to be discussion about the possibility of establishing a fortified position to act as a fixed trading station, as an alternative rendezvous. Another benefit of the expedition was the opportunity which it offered for exploring the interior. One of the participants, Pieter Potter, the surveyor, was given a wide brief to survey the valleys, mountains, hills, waters and rivers, as well as areas of forest and cultivation. There was to be no shooting "because it frightens the natives." Among early reports sent back from the expedition, it was made clear that the oxen were weighed down by all the copper and that there was a need for gunny bags, made of coarse sacking, to carry the load. The corporal who delivered the note to the fort was sent back with the bags and during the journey he encountered three Khoi who reported that the Saldanhars were in four encampments about four days' journey, roughly north-east, by a big river. The expedition named the river the Great Berg River and observed that it passed through the Kloof between Diamand and Paarl on one side and Klapmuts on the other. Having achieved their aim of contact with the Saldanhars, the expedition returned in good heart, bringing seven cows, three calves and forty-one sheep. However, since the Saldanhars needed their cattle for their own livelihood, only a few could be spared for trade on that occasion.

Meanwhile, the voyage of the *Robbejacht* to Saldanha Bay had also been used to lay claim to Dassen Island with a board bearing the Company's name and supported on two poles. The VOC mark was also cut on a large immovable rock on the north side of Saldanha Bay. In order to improve the accuracy of earlier charts, another task for the crew of the *Robbejacht* was to take careful note of depths, grounds, reefs, rocks, sands, shallows, bays and inlets.

The demand for timber increased as new structures were needed to accommodate the growing activities at the Cape. The timber requirements both for construction and for fuel led to the restriction that no timber was to be cut from the Company's forests except by Company servants. Two master craftsmen, who were now freemen, were working in woods behind Table Mountain on the way to the Company's forests, where they made wagons, ploughs, harrows and all kinds of farming equipment. As an example of the growing sense of stability of the community, one of the carpenters, Reoloff Zieuwertssen, was to send to Holland for his wife to come and join him. However, the VOC was perpetually uneasy about the concept of freemen lest they should undermine the workings, and especially the profits, which were of paramount importance to the Company. There was a fine for any freeman who purchased elephant tusks, rhinoceros horns, ostrich feathers or any other goods derived from livestock. It was felt that such practices did not help the all important cattle trade and were a distraction from it. Initially it had been the firm intention of the Company for the settlement at the Cape to be only a stopping place and refreshment haven for the crews of ships on the way to India, but despite the Company's opposition it gradually grew into a colony or settlement.

A colourful reminder is given of the wildness of the countryside and the possibility of encountering a dangerous animal when walking alone in the forest. It suddenly became a reality for one of the Company's most valued craftsmen, Wouter Mostert, who, it was recorded, nearly came to grief when he met a large lion "so close to the beast that he almost collapsed with fright." Fortunately he had the presence of mind to escape by climbing a tree. Earlier that year, 1657, another hazard had presented itself when the journal recorded in graphic detail: "A Hottentot had been bitten by an adder in the foot, which caused it to swell considerably; to prevent the poison spreading, they had bound the leg tightly in two places under the knee and sacrificed the foot as the blood-letters do, and covered it with warm fresh cow dung. A man and a woman, kneeling down, sucked the blood from the cuts and spat it out on the cow dung, with all the eagerness of a child at the breast." Snakes were also in evidence on Robben Island where there were several reports of the need to exterminate them on account of their nuisance value, which included the pursuit of young rabbits inside the burrows.

In the middle of November 1657, there was a welcome visit to the fort by the Chief of the Chainouqua tribe, from the interior, together with a hundred men and seventy one head of cattle which they had brought for a quick sale. These people were the most distant Saldanhars from beyond the Great Berg River. Jan van Riebeeck made sure that the party was given hospitality and quantities of food and brandy were consumed "so that some became rather jolly." This marked a new step in the progress towards enlarging the trading network and finding new supplies of cattle and other important resources.

CHAPTER 4

Hazards of the Sea

In December 1657, when the summer south-easter was blowing with a force that could seriously endanger shipping, two vessels were sighted at some distance from the shore, which they were unable to reach. One eventually managed to anchor near Robben Island and a sloop was despatched to find out the details of its voyage. The sloop returned with the news that one ship was the *Slot van Honingen* and the other the *Arnhem*. Both vessels, on the return from Batavia, were in a bad way with sickness, a severe shortage of food, and storm-damaged equipment. Before either ship could reach the anchorage in Table Bay, there was an exchange of letters with van Riebeeck.

The hazards of navigating and sailing such distances and in such stormy seas were numerous and the problems highlighted were by no means uncommon. The ensuing two-month long exchange of letters between the two ships and the shore are quoted in full as illustrating one of the more dangerous voyages and the appalling conditions endured by the crews on behalf of the relentless VOC.

The first letter is from the officers of the *Honingen* to van Riebeeck, the Commander of the fort, brought ashore by the sloop. It explained the predicament of those on board after a journey of over ten months.

To the Commander of the Fort:
"The ships at present here are the Slot van Honingen *and the* Arnhem. *which left Batavia for the Fatherland on 4 February last in company with the* Henriette Louijse *and the* Avondstar *under*

the flag of the Hon. Volquerus Westerwolt. During May, they encountered such violent westerly winds and storms near the Cape that they would have perished if they had kept on their course. We on the Slot van Honingen *were on 21 May obliged to abandon the voyage home temporarily (God better it) in order to save the crew and the ship with her cargo, and to steer for Mauritius to winter in the north-west haven, where the ships arrived safely on 2 July, glory be to God, though in a very disabled condition and without any drinking water, and with many sick, weak and exhausted men on board.*

Since leaving the Sunda Straits, we saw and heard nothing of the other three ships until we met the Arnhem *on 13th of this month, a little to the east of Cape Agulhas. We learned that the latter vessel had not fared any better and had retreated to Madagascar. She was in need of provisions as well as sails, ropes and other ship's requirements, except rice, of which she had obtained enough at that island for her immediate need. Things would have gone very badly with us if, through the remarkable dispensation of the Lord, the ship* Hof van Zeelandt *coming straight from the Fatherland, and well laden, had not appeared at that island and supplied us with most of the things we need-ed – except bread and rice, of which she only had a limited sup-ply. She was also poorly supplied with sails. Should we be unable to reach the roadstead and the anchors fail us, on account of the bad weather, with the result that we are driven out to sea like the* Arnhem, *which has already disappeared from sight, and we are thereby prevented from calling here, which God forbid, Your Honour is humbly requested to draw the supplies mentioned for both ships from the vessels arriving here, and forward them to us at St. Helena with the next return fleet. We shall otherwise be unable to complete the voyage to the Fatherland, perhaps getting into a worse plight than that which we have already experi-enced. May God preserve us and assist us eventually to reach the longed-for Fatherland safely. To Him we also, in conclusion, recommend Your Honour."*

On board the Slot van Honingen *17 December 1657.*
(Signed) Johan Goosens, Claes Speelman

In response to this desperate and plaintive missive, the sloop was
sent out with food from the fort in the form of a sheep and some
vegetables, together with a reply from the Commander.

To the Hon. Johan Goosens:
"From Your Honour's letter we learn, inter alia, of your painful
voyage and the fact that the other vessel, the Arnhem *is poorly*
supplied with many things, especially anchors and cables,
though well supplied with rice and other foodstuffs. We note fur-
ther that Your Honour, like ourselves, fear that she may have
lost one or two anchors yesterday and probably proceeded to St.
Helena. Furthermore, noting Your Honour's fear that you also
will not be able to reach the roadstead should S.S.E. wind con-
tinue to blow so fiercely, which we hope will not be the case, we
advise you in that case and in accordance with the instructions
of the Lords and Masters which all ships have on board, that it
is possible to reach the anchorage at the Robben Island and the
Dassen Island or at any rate the Saldanha Bay. Skipper J.
Sijmonssen on board Your Honour's ship is well aware of this,
as the charts were drawn from observations made by him and
from information obtained direct from him. But we believe that
the Honingen *will be able to reach the anchorage and will not*
be obliged to leave the bay, as Your Honour is already lying
behind two anchors and it has never happened during our
experience that vessels anchored here have been driven out of
the bay by this wind. The S.S.E. blows from the land and forms
a weather-shore.

We therefore trust that the Arnhem *will still arrive or at least*
reach the Saldanha Bay, so that Your Honour can be supplied
from here with as much as we can give you especially an anchor
and a cable. Your Honour is therefore requested to do your best
in order that the said ship may not remain without the required

assistance and accordingly have to wait here for the return fleet but may be enabled to resume the voyage to the Fatherland sooner, or that another plan may be adopted in the best interests of the Company and for the safety of the ships. In any case, should your Honour be driven away from here or leave after obtaining refreshment, you are to call at the Saldanha Bay to see whether the Arnhem *has put in there. In the event, we request Your Honour to hand over the 20 brass plates and 5 rolls of flat lead on board Your Honour's ship, and also the 20 flat plates of copper in the* Arnhem, *to the men of the* Robbejacht *at that bay, who are extracting oil and catching birds. Should that boat have left, however, Your Honour is requested to bury them on the Schapen Island in that bay, well known to skipper Jan Sijmonssen, with a mark and a letter, where we can find them, so that we may send for them later. Should the* Arnhem *have gone straight to St. Helena, the copper which she has on board is to be buried there, as one of our yachts now cruising off the coast of Angola will shortly touch at St. Helena, so that we may obtain it from there, for it is badly needed here.*
Herewith, etc."
In the Fort of Good Hope, 17 December 1657
(Signed) Jan van Riebeeck

This letter provides a good insight into the trading practices and practicalities involved. Van Riebeeck's careful instructions show how important it was to take safe delivery of vital items. It must have been irksome to van Riebeeck that it was the Company's policy that any commander of a passing ship superseded the authority of the Commander of the fort during his stay in the bay. Later in the day, there were conflicting reports as to whether the *Arnhem* could be seen heading in from the sea on a following wind. In the evening, the Commander himself climbed the Lion's Rump from where he could see the *Arnhem* tacking beyond Robben Island; the wind had again gone round to the south east. In the meantime, the sloop brought back a second letter from the *Honingen*.

To the Commander
"We received Your Honour's letter with the return of the sloop, also the refreshments, which we found to be in accordance with the note. We are very grateful for your kindness and care, and Your Honour can expect the requested 20 plates of copper, but the 5 rolls of flat lead are not to be found on board. Should we be driven away, which we hope will not happen, we shall do with the 20 copper plates in the Arnhem *as it has pleased your Honour to recommend to us. Further, we must correct Your Honour's impression of the position in which both ships find themselves, which we have not described properly or which Your Honour has misunderstood, as the* Arnhem *is not only in need of anchor, cables and other requirements, but is also without any provisions, with the exception of rice, which is the only article of which she obtained a supply at Madagascar, while we on the contrary are fairly well provided with provisions. In addition, 20 or 30 water casks are required, as most of those we have are bad and unfit for use. If, therefore, Your Honour cannot provide the vessels with the above, we shall be obliged to await the arrival of a ship from the Fatherland or of the return fleet from Batavia."*
The Slot van Honingen *17 December 1657.*
(Signed) Johan Goosens, Claes Speelman

After considering the two missives from the *Honingen*, the Council of Policy resolved to supply both ships with their needs in order that the Company should not be further inconvenienced by the delay of the ships bringing such valuable cargoes. However, it was obviously recognised that the Cape settlement could be in danger of finding itself short of supply until the next fleet arrived. On the following day, 18 December, the south-south-easterly wind blew hard again and the sloop made ready to take further provisions to the *Slot van Honingen* together with a further letter from the Commander, somewhat reluctantly agreeing to the demands of the ships:

To the Hon. Johan Goosens
"We received Your Honour's second letter last night on the return of our sloop and from it we fully learned of your requirements. We have decided to provide these two valuable ships with what they require from our slender resources, so that they need not wait for outward bound ships or ships returning from India, even if we have in consequence to suffer privation for a while, as the speedy arrival of these ships is of great importance to the Hon. Company. On reaching the anchorage, please make a list of all Your Honour's requirements, with the quantities and description, and transmit it to us. As regards the water casks also, we hope to be able to assist Your Honour, if the iron hoops of your old casks have been preserved.

Yesterday towards evening, having ascended the Lion Mountain, I sighted the Arnhem *under sail just below Robben Island. We therefore trust that she will be able to reach the roadstead to be provided with what she needs, as she has obtained a good supply of rice at Madagascar, while according to your second letter Your Honour is also fairly well supplied with other provisions. We will do our best even if, as stated, we have to deprive ourselves for a while and suffer privation until the arrival of the ships from the Fatherland, rather than detain Your Honour at great cost to the Company and to the detriment of its interests. If we hoist the flag it will be a sign to Your Honour that we have again sighted the* Arnhem. *Your Honour must please do the same if you see her before we do.*

We are sending as much refreshment for the men and greens for Your Honour's saloon as the small boat can carry, also three fresh loaves for your Honour and the ladies. Milk can only be obtained from the free farmers, a distance of about one and a half hour's walk, which is too far away, and it can moreover not be taken over in our small sloop in this windy weather. Herewith, etc."
In the Fort of Good Hope, 18 December 1657.
(Signed) Jan van Riebeeck

The sloop took this letter and some more provisions out to the *Honingen* in increasingly stormy conditions. The *Honingen* could still see the *Arnhem* and hoisted her flag in the stern to indicate this although the *Arnhem* could not be seen from the shore. The next morning, the south-easter continued to blow with force until midday after which the sloop was able to return safely to the shore bearing a third, more optimistic letter from the officers of the *Honingen*.

> *To the Commander of the Fort:*
> "*We perused Your Honour's second letter, received by the sloop this morning. We are now relieved from the fears we expressed and we learn with great joy that you hope to be able to assist us and the* Arnhem *with the most necessary requirements to enable us to resume the voyage soon, so that we shall not have to wait here for ships from the Fatherland or India. We are very pleased about this. Thereby Your Honour will render the Company a great service. When by the grace of God we reach the roads safely, we shall furnish Your Honour with a list of things required by us, and further communicate with you orally about all matters as circumstances require. We are grateful for the greens again sent us, and for the fresh loaves.*
>
> *The* Arnhem *is still visible from the topmast, but she is so far away to sea that she can barely be discerned. She is evidently lying to, waiting for more favourable weather and wind. Like Your Honour we hope that she will be able to come here. Herewith, etc.*"
> *In the* Slot van Honingen *18 December 1657.*

A postscript made a desperate plea for material to mend the top-sail:

> "*NB. Hon. Sir, we are badly in need of a topsail. Should the one we are using at the moment give way, we should be in great distress, and we should therefore be obliged if Your Honour would*

*send us a bale of Dutch canvas by boat as soon as possible, so
that the sail-makers can be put to work at once; also some tar –
of which we have none whatsoever - for the windings around
the topmast, which is beginning to show cracks."
(Signed) Johan Goosens.*

After the receipt of this further request, the sloop set out once
more with further fresh provisions and the tar. However, gale
force winds again developed and the sloop was delayed, not able
to return until the 20th, bringing a short note to van Riebeeck,
expressing gratitude.

To the Commander
*"As directed in Your Honour's letter, the quartermaster deliv-
ered everything to us in good order and we again thank you
heartily. We had hoped that the wind would have turned and
helped us today, but it has gone back to its old quarter; If, however, Your Honour remains so mindful of us, it would be better
rather to stay here than to rove about the seas. For the rest we
must trust in God."*
In the Slot van Honingen. *19 December 1657.*
(Signed) Jan Goosens.

The saga continued and the following day the gales had finally
reduced to a breeze. After sailing for four hours, the *Honingen* was
able to anchor in the roadstead. On arrival, the senior merchant,
Johan Goosens, and the skipper of the ship landed and handed
the Commander a list of their chief needs. The quantity and variety of their requirements were a clear indication of the depriva-
tions which the *Honingen* had suffered on her ten-month voyage
from the East. The precise list included the following:

*1 heavy anchor; 1 heavy cable; 2 anchor stocks; 1 piece stand-
ing rigging; 6 puddenings for main rigging with 6 dead-eyes; 1
new rope for downhauls; 1 ditto for tackle and rigging; 2 coils
of rope for the running rigging; 12 lines of 9,12,and 15; 12*

bandies of house line; 12 bundles of marline; 3 or 4 large hooks with covers for the tackle; 6 puddening bolts; 26 water casks; six and a half lasts of rice; 2 aums of oil of olives; 1 leaguer of vinegar; 1 aum train-oil; 2 casks tar; one and a half casks pitch; 3 large scrapers for cleaning the ships; 1 piece old cable for oakum; 6 rolls Dutch canvas for the main topsail (should there be none of the Dutch kind, then 325 ells French canvas will do; for the mizzen, 220 ells Dutch canvas; for the foresail, 430 ells Dutch canvas; 25 strands twine; 8 or 10 bundles of cane.
Done this day on board the Slot van Honingen, *20 December (Signed) Claes Speelman*

On the following day, an unseasonal change in the midsummer weather brought a north west wind and driving rain. This enabled the beleaguered *Arnhem* to approach the Table Bay anchorage before nightfall after sheltering near Dassen Island in an attempt to avoid the worst of the storms. Van Riebeeck's journal records that among her crew, there were not more than ten men in good health, while thirty seven men had died on the voyage so far. A variety of fresh food was urgently sent on board as a first step towards improving the health and well-being of the crew. In the morning of 22 December, the officers of the *Arnhem* came ashore and described their predicament in more detail. All were said to be suffering from dropsy; among those who had died were two skippers, so the chief mate had been in charge of the ship.

On Christmas Eve, the Broad Council, made up of the Council of Policy and representatives of the two ships, reiterated the previous decision that the *Slot van Honingen* and the *Arnhem* should be supplied with their needs as speedily as possible in order to minimise further delays in their journey to Holland. The cargo of the *Arnhem* was listed as the more valuable of the two ships at eight hundred thousand guilders, whereas the *Honingen* was valued at three hundred thousand guilders. Some time was spent in deliberating how best to replace the skippers who had died on the voyage. After a further exchange of views, it was decided that skipper

Claes Speelman should be transferred from the *Honingen* to the *Arnhem* and that skipper Sijmonssen Clos should be appointed to the *Honingen*. On 26 December, all the sick on the *Arnhem* were brought ashore and put in hospital to be restored to health. Because of the weak state of the *Arnhem* crew, no immediate decision could be taken with regard to the fixing of a sailing date. Since the crew, over 150 of them, were in such urgent need of bread, some one thousand eight hundred pounds of 'bread' or biscuit were taken from the *Honingen* for the purpose, while the *Arnhem*, being well-stocked with Madagascar rice, was able to give the *Honingen* three thousand six hundred pounds of it in exchange.

By 7 January 1658, many of the *Arnhem* company were gaining better health though there were still seventeen or eighteen in hospital. The Commander was getting anxious to agree a date for the departure of the two vessels but it was still considered to be premature both on the grounds of health and, as yet, of the uncertain food supplies for the long voyage ahead. A week later, a change of plan took place when Claes Speelman was allowed to remain on the *Honingen* and Sijmonssen Clos was instructed to command the *Arnhem* instead. There was no further discussion of sailing dates until 30 January when a Broad Council meeting resolved that in the continued absence of a well-stocked supply ship, it would be unwise for the *Arnhem* to leave. It was reckoned that the *Honingen* might sail on alone but that in practice it would be too risky. All this forced inactivity bred resentment among the crews. On 12 February, the captains of the two ships went ashore with the complaint that they had only enough 'bread' or biscuit and rice for two days. The Council were already aware of acute shortages on the *Arnhem* and it was decided to transfer two casks of salt pork from the *Honingen*. This was not the end of the problem and a serious dispute ensued.

On the following day, the officers of the *Arnhem* reported that the *Honingen* had refused to hand over the pork, in spite of the ship having twelve or thirteen casks as well as other meat. The crew of the *Honingen* were firmly told by the Commander that until they handed over the casks of pork they would be allowed no further supplies from the Company's stores. When another day passed and Speelman came ashore without having handed over the pork, the Commander upbraided him for his lack of leadership over a truculent crew. It transpired that the butler's mate was the cause of all the trouble. He had said that he "did not care a fig for the Council or anybody" and had flatly refused to open the hold, defying anyone to take the keys off him. After they had stirred up more trouble, the mate and other ringleaders were brought before the Commander. The mate was locked up in the fort and the Commander eventually dispersed the supporters who had followed him to the fort and who had "displayed great hostility and created a great disturbance." At long last, on 18 February, the *Shelvis* arrived from Batavia after a six week voyage. She was well supplied with victuals intended for the Cape but much was to be diverted to the *Honingen* and the *Arnhem*. Further supplies were provided through the Council to ensure that the two ships had an ample quantity for what could be a five-month voyage to Holland. There were 150 men on the *Arnhem*, who were unnerved by their previous experiences on their way to the Cape, so it was important for morale that the ship should be seen to be fully stocked with food for a long voyage.

Heading for St. Helena, where they hoped to meet the homeward bound fleet, which appeared to have by-passed the Cape, the *Honingen* and the *Arnhem* eventually sailed on the afternoon of 23 February 1658 and reached open sea by nightfall, after spending ten weeks at Table Bay. As a result of the long sojourn in port of the two ships, it was estimated that forty cattle and fifty sheep had been consumed so a new expedition to the Saldanhars was planned to trade for stock to replenish supplies. Sergeant Jan van Hawarden and fifteen "wide awake" men made ready with rations for a three-week expedition, taking with them copper, tobacco, and pipes "to see if a goodly number of cattle can be bought from them on friendly terms."

A month after setting out for the interior, the expedition returned triumphantly having discovered the pass "over the mountain range of Africa against which the Berg River lies." This was the Tulbagh Basin, which became important in the following century. However, the bartering aspect of the trip was not successful because the expedition party saw only a few Khoi and no Saldanhars.

CHAPTER 5

Slaves, Freemen and Burghers

The year 1658 was the year of the first arrival at the Cape of slaves by the shipload. In February, the *Amersfoot* intercepted a Portuguese slaver bound from Angola to the Bay Tote la Sanctos on the coast of Brazil laden with five hundred male and female slaves. The *Amersfoot* took off half this number and left the rest in the Portuguese ship, which was "old and unserviceable." By the time the *Amersfoot* reached Table Bay on 28 March, the number of slaves had been reduced to one hundred and seventy. Many had died and others were ill. They were brought ashore to start their new lives having been, as far as possible, restored to health. Van Riebeeck's journal observed "the majority of the slaves are young boys and girls who will be of little use for the next four or five years."

A second shipload of slaves arrived six weeks later in the *Hasselt* from the Gulf of Guinea, having left Popo, Dahomey, on 22 February with two hundred and seventy one male and female slaves. Of these forty three died on the voyage, so that two hundred and twenty eight slaves arrived at the Cape where they were landed on 7 May, noted in the journal as: "an exceptionally fine, strong and lively lot." Thus there were nearly four hundred slaves at the Cape. This first importation of slaves from Angola and the East Indies were to perform the labour which the San and the Khoi refused to do. From the start, the Company's policy had been to ban making slaves of the local people, mostly because the Dutch settlers were afraid of jeopardising their cattle trade with the Khoi and other tribes. There was no indigenous slavery at the Cape and the local chiefs did not have the power nor the population to engage in the slave trade. Soon after his arrival, van Riebeeck had asked the Council of Seventeen for a labour force of slaves but was told, surprisingly, that none could be spared. With all the new slave arrivals, he now had more than he could cope with and he planned to send a number on to India. To this end, the *Hasselt* was made ready to carry up to two hundred slaves on to Batavia, leaving just over two hundred slaves at the Cape.

Later, arrangements were made to set up a school for the Company's slaves who had been brought to the Cape from Angola in the *Amersfoot*. The school was the first to be established in South Africa and had morning and afternoon sessions taught by the 'sick-comforter,' Pieter van der Stael. A curious bribe was attached to the educational arrangements: "To encourage the slaves to attend school and to hear or learn Christian prayers, it is ordered that after school everyone is to receive a small glass of brandy and two inches of tobacco". The slaves were to be properly clothed against the approaching winter. It was recorded that the strongest of the slaves had already been put to work so that they would "as soon as possible be of use to the settlement". There were, however, no signs of a Company policy to convert the slaves to Protestantism.

By degrees, the slaves working at the Cape formed two categories, some employed by the VOC on public works and housed in a slave lodge near the fort, while others belonged to individual burghers and farmers. Feeding so large a number might have been a serious problem but for the fact that the slaves appeared content with a diet of dried, salted meat, eggs and birds, including penguins. Supplies of this food came largely from coastal trade with Saldanha Bay and neighbouring islands, which had the advantage of presenting no competition to food supplies needed by the European settlers. Employment of the slaves was mainly in those categories where van Riebeeck felt under pressure due to a shortage of labour. Ploughing, sowing, wood-sawing and fishing were among the leading occupations soon to involve slaves, both by the VOC and by the freemen, while a whole group were put to work in the Company's gardens. It was not long, however, before desertions became a common topic in van Riebeeck's journal.

Early in June 1658, it was noted that the previous night five male and two female Angolan slaves had deserted, one from the forest, two from the fort and two pairs from the Company's grain fields. They had been among the first to arrive, and had been incited to it by the oldest slave from the forest, who had pretended that he was ill and accordingly had come to the fort and along the way had visited the slaves at the Company's grain fields. "Shortly after midnight, the three had left the fort and had been joined the next morning by those from the grain fields, evidently at a signal given to one another in passing. Men were immediately sent out in all directions to look for the deserters, including some Hottentots, who were encouraged by the promise of large rewards if they brought the fugitives back and were given tobacco and bread in advance to take with them on the journey." Ten days later, a group of Khoi who were visiting the fort said that their women had seen some of the runaway Angola slaves on the coast between the Cape settlement and Saldanha Bay but their menfolk had been unable to find them and bring them back. A week later, the freeman Casper Brinkman came to report that all four of his Guinea slaves had deserted during the night, taking some rice and clothing with them. The freeman maintained that the slaves had never been ill-treated, locked up, or beaten: "our men are unable to pursue them because of their fleetness of foot, and the seven runaway Angola slaves of the Company have hitherto not been recaptured." It was suspected that the Khoi were helping the deserting slaves to maintain some sort of independence, since Khoi women had often been seen giving the slaves broiled tortoises and other food, and beckoning to them and pointing towards the Leopard Mountain.

The Council of Policy took a hand in the matter of slave behaviour, and on 29 June passed sentence on the runaway male and female slaves who had been recovered, as follows: "All are to be tied to a post in the open and scourged; one is to be branded, whilst two are to be placed in chains, linked to each other, until their masters request that they be set free, as stated more fully in the sentences." This level of treatment was in marked contrast to the friendlier attitude which the Seventeen were anxious the Dutch settlers should adopt towards the Khoi. In mid-August, two slaves of the free fisherman Maerten Jochumssen deserted, and Khoi were at once sent in pursuit of them but the pursuers later reported no sign of the missing slaves. At the end of the month, the Commander made a tour of inspection of freemen and their work where he learned that fourteen male and female slaves of the free sawyers had deserted overnight. Two female slaves were recovered, who made known by signs that their men-folk had intended to cut the throats of the tree sawyers during the night while they were asleep if they could only have got hold of knives. Unrest spread to the gardens where two of the Company's slaves had also absconded during the night, after breaking out of the building outside the fort in which they had been locked up.

The Europeans became anxious both on account of the interruption to work and because a group of twenty eight fugitive slaves were forming a formidable group. "They are sharper, much bolder and braver than the Hottentots, and will multiply in the course of time and the Hon. Company will have good cause to fear them more than the natives." Desertions were to continue and fourteen slaves ran away a few days later notwithstanding the fact that each had a chain on his leg with an iron ball at the end. With expertise, the slaves became adept at removing the fetters and two of the Commander's slaves who had escaped were brought back without chains. It was found that at the Company's grain fields they had conspired with others, who had chains on their legs, to kill the Company's servants there, and then run away in a large troop.

Another Guinea slave, when asked what they would have lived on, had replied that they would have relied on subsisting on the flesh of Khoi, whom they would have killed here and there, as they were accustomed to in their own country, where the victor ate the conquered. They said they had enough knives to kill the first Khoi, which on investigation was found to be true, for some had as many as nine and none, including the women, were without knives, which they had stolen and collected. The Guinea slaves were thus seen to pose a serious threat in their bids for freedom since they were bold and resourceful. It was clear that they would have to be more closely guarded and a better watch was provided over the slaves who believed that they would be able to reach their own country in due course. Some of them had even planned to seize a boat which belonged to one of the ships and which was being used for fishing in the river or near the beach; they intended to make off with it, searching for their country by sailing along the coast. To augment the labour force, slaves were later imported in large numbers from the East Indies, Ceylon and Madagascar.

On July 5, 1658, a significant event took place. Following negotiations for peace with the Khoi, a long list of treaty conditions was construed. This was the first agreement to be drawn up between Europeans and native inhabitants but it proved to be no more successful than many subsequent treaties. Van Riebeeck's journal observed: "The native, whose conceptions of moral obligations differed radically from those of the Europeans, did not understand what was expected of him and did not regard himself as irrevocably bound by these treaties." On the following day, the journal gave the first report of a mixed marriage. Jan Sacharies of Amsterdam became engaged to a former slave girl, Maria, whose place of birth had been Bengal. She was brought into freedom by her fiancé for the purpose of marriage. It was noted with approval that she spoke Dutch fluently and already "had a fair knowledge of Christ according to the Reformed religion." The marriage was to be conducted in the council chamber by the council secretary.

There are many other tales recorded in the diary of the lives and activities of slaves and early freemen. The Company at this time released a number of its servants, mostly sailors and soldiers, to become free burghers and farmers to help in herding cattle and growing crops on its behalf, while they had to keep to strict rules on marketing their produce.

From a reckoning of the Company's financial assets and cattle trading, it was shown that a certain Khoi miscreant, Harry, had behaved dishonestly, so his possessions had been deducted from the Company's debt to him. The VOC had told Harry that they did not intend to return anything to him because the amount that had been recovered from him was less than the Company would have gained from the extra livestock he should have provided. A few days later Harry was locked up on Robben Island and it became apparent that no native had pleaded on behalf of Harry, except Eva, his niece, a Khoi servant of the Dutch. However, a diary entry noted that she believed he did not wish to return, preferring to spend the rest of his life on Robben Island in peace since his fellow countrymen all hated him and wished to kill him.

The poor state of the Company's pig population was highlighted in the journal. Twenty one sows and boars "small and large, sick and healthy, lame and cripple" were to be looked after by Jannekin Boddijs, whose husband was the sergeant at the fort. Pig meat was evidently an important source of food for the Cape community but no-one was allowed to kill more than one pig a year since it was obligatory to deliver everything to the VOC at the price already fixed. To prevent them going through hedges and damaging the gardens, the pigs had to wear triangular collars, but these proved to be more cumbersome than effective and after a time they were given up. The journal commented that the rearing of pigs was much more successful in private hands and at no cost to the Company. In order to control the animals properly "every owner of pigs, however small his herd, shall keep a slave or Dutch servant to keep the pigs out of the enclosed gardens as far as possible, while driving them to and from home, and to prevent them from breaking out at night."

An anecdote in the journal recorded that the career of the stalwart Wouter Mostert had been enhanced when the mill was granted to him since he was a good industrious sober man, married to an industrious woman who strove to get on. However, in a manner typical of the VOC's strict bureaucracy, Mostert was not allowed to grind corn for the freemen because "all the wheat and rye was to remain at the Company's disposal." Among Mostert's other accomplishments, it was noted that he was a good tile maker and brick maker. Bricks were sold at five guilders per thousand to the Company and at six guilders per thousand to the burghers.

An important resolution was passed on 20 August 1658 with regard to the number of cattle available to freemen. The increase of cattle was the chief object of the VOC and other freemen were not to receive cattle until the farmers themselves were properly provided for. Meanwhile, a record of the occupations of the other freemen indicated the extent to which economic activity had widened after six years of European development at the Cape. There were now fishermen, tailors, millers, hunters, bakers, carpenters and sawyers, all of whom were prospering through their hard work. They were allowed to breed pigs, tend gardens, keep fowls, geese, ducks, turkeys, and bees and do anything else they might like to. Every farmer was to have six good cows in calf in addition to his draught oxen. Farmers with wives and children were to have twelve cattle to help make a better living from milk and butter.

On 21 August that year, the Commander set about planting vines on his farm at Boscheuvel. This was a firm step forward in the development of a branch of cultivation that was to assume great importance later in the century. The freemen were unwilling to plant vines on their own lands because "they were not in a position to plant them or because of ignorance." Within a week, the Commander had twelve hundred rooted branches and cuttings from the vines at Boscheuvel, while the original stocks were left standing in the Company's gardens.

Meanwhile, there were continuing problems with the slaves from the Dutch point of view following the desertion of fourteen more male and female slaves. Moreover, "Doman the interpreter is a rascal and tries hard to thwart the Hon. Company in everything and is thrice as bad and harmful as Harry ever was, as we discover daily." Eva, the Khoi girl, who had been trained in domestic service by the Commander's wife, was something of an informant and declared openly that Doman was the chief enemy of the Company. In return, he called her a "lickspittle or flatterer" and made her seem odious among her own people by saying that she spoke more in favour of the Dutch than the Khoi. Van Riebeeck wished this scamp could be seized without causing unrest and removed to Robben Island. Two days later, it was decreed that the slaves should be put in irons to prevent escapes.

At the end of September, it was briefly noted that five male and one female slaves had died that month. A cavalier attitude towards the slaves, which was not peculiar to the Dutch, was evident from the journal. It reported that the Company slaves numbered eighty three among whom were thirty four men and forty nine women who were mostly old and useless and about thirty were mad, ill or crippled and could be of no particular service. "We shall be relieved of this burden however as they will soon die off."

Glimpses of everyday life and husbandry evoked a picture of the ups and downs of the developing community. In October 1658, concern was expressed at the misuse of the unallocated forest lands which were being "recklessly destroyed." Too much timber was being cut down unnecessarily and left to decay. People were taking more than they needed and selling it at high prices to the English and the brick makers. It was recorded in the diary that the draught oxen were thoroughly exhausted and no-one showed the least signs of gratitude to the VOC to which the wood actually belonged. Two free sawyers had taken their discharge for fifteen years and each was allocated a part of the forest from which they were to supply planks and all kinds of timber. The monopoly thus

set up was to regularise the felling and supply of timber, so that
those requiring timber or other wood, including spars and slats,
would be able to buy what they wanted at a reasonable price from
these sawyers. The planting of fruit and vegetable crops was to be
carried out so as to be ready to supply the winter ships and the
return ships from Batavia with an abundance of refreshments.

The making of beer was among the accomplishments of the community, and it was noted that the beer was rising nicely in the
cooler and it had begun to ferment well. More was to be brewed
so that some casks could be sent to Batavia and Holland to test
how long it would remain in good condition at sea. Later in
October that year, there were entries concerning the increased
well-being of the farming community: "All the agriculturists are
now adequately provided with draught oxen and milch cows and
each family has at least fifty sheep." However, the usual problem
of keeping pigs featured once more: "everyone is unwilling to
keep pigs because of the great trouble and expense it involves."

A most unexpected event occurred to surprise the whole community, with the sudden appearance from overland of three men from
the ship *West Vrieslandt*, which had anchored in Saldanha Bay, in a
desolate condition and full of sick men. The crew had no strength
to weigh anchor; one hundred and fifty cases of scurvy were
brought ashore and seventy two had already died. An urgent letter
to van Riebeeck, brought by the overland party, said that they had
been at sea with a crew of three hundred and fifty one men, very
few of whom were still in good health. "We have no doubt that Your
Honour will provide us with succour which we eagerly await." The
Council immediately resolved to dispatch the *Schapenjacht* with a
supply of carrots, beet, turnips, horse and Spanish radishes, and as
much milk and as many eggs as could be hurriedly collected from
the freemen. The *West Vrieslandt* was urged to get to Table Bay as
soon as possible. The following day, van Riebeeck wrote:

"*We have filled our boat the* Schapenjacht *with the following durable fruits, etc. including nine bags carrots, ten bags turnips, thirty bags horse and Spanish radishes, fifty artichokes as a delicacy for the saloon, forty five bunches of leeks and garlick, thirty five cans of milk in a cask, five hundred and sixty four fresh hens' and ducks' eggs in a large and small cask, both open and filled with sand, for the sick and the saloon and also six live sheep."*

A few days later, the *West Vrieslandt* arrived in the roadstead with its crew in better health. It was surely a remarkable achievement that such a quantity of provisions should have been gathered together so quickly.

A further vivid reminder of the presence of wild animals and the need to be on guard against them occurred on 25 October, when a lion carried off a draught ox and "ate four or five pounds of meat from the rump." It was recorded that three sheep were eaten by a lion near the VOC granary and that the herds themselves were in some danger. A lion also killed a cow in the kraal (stock enclosure) at night, disturbed the herd and caused a general alarm. A more spectacular encounter with a lion was reported in detail in the journal. During the forenoon, the Commander, walking in the gardens, had seen tracks of wild beasts everywhere, and shortly afterwards a bold lion jumped up just outside the gardens not more than forty or fifty paces from him, and leisurely made off towards Table Mountain. The sergeant and the huntsman, with four or five soldiers, were sent after it with firelocks, and fully two hundred Khoi followed immediately, driving all their sheep and cattle. They cornered the lion in a deep 'kloof' or ravine on the slopes of Table Mountain, so that its only way of escape was by breaking through the sheep which the Khoi had placed in front of them "as a breastwork for their defence." The lion had lain hidden under a bush and the Khoi stood outside the flock of sheep and between them and the cattle. Whenever the lion showed itself and, roaring, tried to break out and seize a sheep, they hurled their 'assegais' or spears at it over the sheep, with great noise and shouting, at which the lion retreated. "It was a very singular spectacle. As the Hottentots could not hit it, the sergeant, who was with our huntsmen and others, about eight or ten paces away from the lion, fired first but missed, whereupon the huntsman sent three bullets through its head, an excellent shot, causing it to drop dead at once."

Curiosity about the whereabouts of the inhabitants of the interior was strong among the settlers. The desperate need to develop a more secure meat trade caused an expedition to be formed and, led by Jan van Hawarden, seventeen soldiers set out to find the Chief of the Cochoquas, in the first expedition to use a wagon. The party included Eva, the Khoi, as interpreter, whose sister was the principal wife of Oedasoa, the Chief of the Cochoquas. The family connection was auspicious for trade and the expedition returned cheerfully after five days with over two hundred sheep and twenty five head of cattle. One hundred of the sheep and seven of the cattle came from Eva's brother-in-law and the rest from Ngonomoa, the first captain of his tribe, whose cattle were numerous and therefore regularly on the move to find new pastures because of the amount of grass they consumed daily.

An interesting light was shed on the continuing social problems with which the Company was faced. A notice was issued on 11 November, which read: "To prevent the desertion of freemen, so injurious to the interests of the Hon. Company because of the heavy debts which they leave behind, no freeman, his servants nor his slaves shall in future be allowed to go on board any vessel except with written permission under the Commander's own signature."

Early in December 1658, van Riebeeck went to the grain fields near Rondebosch to see how the harvest was progressing. He found all the men hard at work. His vineyard on the Boscheuvel was growing well and made an encouraging sight which he hoped would inspire others. Early in 1659 "wine was made for the first time from Cape grapes from the new must fresh from the Vat."

The grapes were mainly Muscadel and other white round "fragrant and tasty" grapes. It was, however, to be many years before the Cape wine was to become memorable for its quality.

Another example of the VOC jealousy in guarding the trade of its goods related to salt production. On 13 December 1658, the Council decided to hand over to the free Saldanhar traders for a trial period all the saltpans at the Cape, big and small, wherever they were situated, on condition that they would gather all the salt obtainable from the pans cleanly, high and dry, into heaps. These were to be covered with mats to prevent the salt from melting, so that it could be used the whole year round. Predictably, the Company pointed out that the free traders would not be allowed to sell, present or supply salt to anyone except to the VOC to which it belonged as the Master of the land.

The greater success of breeding sheep on Robben Island led to the provision of timber from the mainland for a shed and kraal. The *Schapenjacht* made several visits to the island over a period of weeks and the Commander went across on the last voyage to see what was going on. He found over four hundred sheep in good condition but there was "no grass anywhere on the island as it was the dry season." It was the responsibility of two slaves on the island to chop wood and take it to the Beacon Hill, where a fire was to be lit whenever ships approached.

CHAPTER 6

Van Riebeeck's Later Years

At the beginning of February 1659, an important expedition was planned which would be away for three months. A memorandum provided the names of the tribes which the members of the expedition were most likely to meet. The Kaapmans, one of the Khoi tribes to which the exiled Harry belonged, had a Chief named Congosoa, also known as the 'Fat Captain.' The two tribes of the Gorachaucqua, known to the Dutch as the 'tobacco thieves', kept to the same area because they dared not confront the powerful true Saldanhars. The Saldanhars were divided into two groups, the Cochoquas and the Khonaiquas. The former were made up of two large and strong groups ruled by Ngonomoa and Oedasoa, the husband of Eva's sister. Both groups had large herds of cattle whose breeding dominated their way of life. The Khonaiquas, also expert cattle breeders, were friendly with the Cochoquas, and lived near them. In addition to the information on the tribes they might meet, the explorers were given a list of instructions concerning specific studies they were to make on the journey. As a result, knowledge of the Cape hinterland would spread to others. There were six main points:

1. to note compass directions;
2. to note clayey soil or arable land, sandy or stony soil or mountainous country, presence of rivers, etc, minerals, and whether the route could take wagons; enquire the names of people and chiefs;
3. to note what tribes subsist on and their whole way of life; discuss their trading needs;
4. to note edible fruit or root crops and 'If you ever come to the coast, mark all bays and river mouths';

5. to discover the nature of settlements and equipment for waging war; ascertain strengths of tribes and who are their friends and enemies;

6. to find out attitudes towards the Dutch; and to study an enclosed memo from the Lords Seventeen on the writing of reports.

From time to time, key figures in the community were singled out for comment, sometimes to record an untimely death. One such occasion was the death of Jan van Hawarden when the Company lost its building supervisor and general superintendent of works and trades after an illness of no more than six or seven days. He left a widow and five children.

The hazards linked with the fierce south-easter winds included not only their tendency to flatten exposed crops but also the risk of fire. A fire was started on one occasion by cow dung set alight by smokers in the kraal. The blaze finally reached the thatch of the new cow-shed and flames shot out of the roof, since the grass was extremely dry after the summer heat. Not many days later, the Commander received news that his house or farmstead on the Boscheuvel had been burnt to the ground by a fire which started inside it.

Occasionally the journal recorded disputes between members of ships' crews. At the end of March 1659, contrary winds delayed the departure of the *Ulisses* and two other vessels. The skipper of the *Ulisses* complained to the Broad Council about his helmsman and the two of them eventually came to blows. The matter was resolved by making the helmsmen of the *Ulisses* and the *Leonen* change places.

Infringement of the Company's rules on trading was a frequently reported problem. The free Saldanhar traders on Dassen Island had been very successful at breeding pigs and had bought up most of the pigs of the free burghers, who had found them difficult to rear. The traders, however, sold them to ships which were calling at Saldanha Bay and at Dassen Island and not at the Cape. Among such ships were those of the English, who would have seen no need to conform with VOC trading regulations laid down for VOC ships. At some stage, the fiscal on Dassen Island had checked up on the pig population, suspecting that all might not be as it should. Van Riebeeck noted that, instead of forty or fifty pigs as they had imagined there would be, he had found only twenty on Dassen Island. According to the free burghers, four had been sold to the yacht *Melkiskerken* and the rest of the pigs had died young. But these twenty were flourishing and most of them were with young, so it was hoped that the numbers would increase.

In May 1659, a petition was presented to the Commander from eighteen free farmers, fishermen, burghers and others with the request that "we may revenge ourselves thoroughly on the Kaapmans tribe and make good our losses, since they have so reduced our stock that we no longer have enough animals to pull our ploughs. According to Your Honour's orders, we are not allowed to treat them otherwise than with kindliness, which is most vexing because they are always causing trouble and loss, chiefly by stealing our cattle and sheep." Less than a fortnight later, a Resolution was passed by the Council of Policy, which recognised that a state of war existed between the European settlers and the Kaapmans. An extract declared: "Since we see no other means of securing peace or tranquillity with these Cape people, we shall take the first opportunity practicable to attack them with a large force and, if possible, take them by surprise. We shall avoid as far as possible, all murderous bloodshed. The prisoners we shall keep as hostages, so that we may restrain and bring to submission those who may evade us. By this means we hope to restore peace, the more so because we feel sure that the true Saldanhars, enemies of the Kaapmans, will care as little about their fate as they did in Harry's case but will more freely come to deal with us in greater security than before, since these Kaapmans have always been found to be the chief hindrance to us."

On the same day, it was recorded that the Commander asked Eva to interrogate some Kaapmans around the fort. "They are actually spies, though we simulate ignorance of this. No-one need imagine that tempers would be improved if we took hostile action; they would rather grow worse and more bitter, for the natives would in revenge do us every injury they could devise."

In view of all these problems, it was hardly surprising that farming was everywhere at a standstill and being neglected since no-one dared to go into the fields to plough or do anything else, which, since it was the rainy season, was to their great detriment. Ten days later, on 31 May 1659, the diary read: "On seeing the preparations made to mount guns for their protection in the countryside, the free burghers seemed to be much encouraged."

Early in June, bad weather prevented contact with "the marauding Hottentots." But the diary noted: "with the coming of fine weather, we trust that we shall come face to face with them, and may the Lord be on our side." Indeed, the month of June, like May before it, saw persistent attacks by the Khoi on cattle and sheep, led by Doman. Twenty Khoi captured from Hendrik Boom, the freeman head gardener, all thirty of his cattle and thirty four sheep. The animals had been grazing on Devil's Peak and the Commander had criticised Boom for allowing his cattle to roam too far from his neighbours' animals.

The journal mentioned deaths among the Company's livestock, in addition to thefts of the burghers' cattle, war, and murders committed by the "barbarous people of this country." In future, a service of intercession and prayer was to be held every Wednesday afternoon at 4 o'clock, so that by prayer and supplication they hoped to avert the wrath of God and gain and keep the upper hand and restore peace and friendly relations with the Khoi.

June continued to be a turbulent month: Doman and fifty or sixty Khoi attacked both the Company's and freeman Harman's draught oxen, while there was a wider attack on cattle. The Khoi were driven off by shots but were unharmed. An attempt had been made to secure greater safety for the cattle and sheep of the Company and of the free burghers by housing them in a kraal next to the Company's granary. The Chief of the Saldanhars, Oedasoa and his assistant Chief Ngonomoa, did not trust the Kaapmans and were interested to know how the Dutch settlers had fared with them. It transpired that Oedasoa had found them unreliable "since the scoundrels were unaccustomed to keeping the peace for long, not being able to live or remain content without committing robbery or murder." They were known to have attacked others when they were at their weakest and Oedasoa himself had experienced such attacks, after he had been beaten by another tribe from far inland. At this point, the Kaapmans had not only robbed him of most of his remaining cattle but had killed and ruthlessly murdered all who could not defend themselves, even women and children; they had even slit open the pregnant women and trampled on unborn children. This had happened shortly before the Dutch came to the Cape. Oedasoa hoped henceforth to establish free access in peace and amity and trade with Hollanders and so supplant these 'mischievous rogues'.

Another instance of van Riebeeck's increasing irritation with his countrymen was typified by the way in which seven free burghers attempted to recapture the freeman Brinkman's cattle. They were driven back by the band of Khoi, about twenty in number, who had been responsible for the theft. Out of sheer carelessness, most of these free burghers had armed themselves with nothing else but pitchforks, only two or three of them carrying firearms. This reverse, due to their own negligence, was taken advantage of by the Khoi. Doman in particular, had been urging them on to all these misdeeds. A reward had been promised for his person, one hundred guilders alive and fifty guilders dead, women and children at half these sums. Three others besides Brinkman lost stock and the Kaapmans had stolen in all sixty eight head of cattle, young and old, and sixty seven sheep and completely ruined their farming. A characteristic VOC comment followed: "To assist them in getting their farming under way again this season would be extremely difficult, for the Company can at present ill-afford any cattle from its stock, which at present consists only of cows and very young bulls incapable of doing work."

The growing enmity of the Khoi was confirmed, however, when Doman admitted that they were "dissatisfied that the Europeans had taken possession of their land" and that he had encouraged the Khoi to set fire to their houses and the grain and to attempt to overpower the fort. Van Riebeeck had requested Batavia to send some horses so that his men could pursue the "fleet-footed" Khoi. One Sunday, towards the end of July 1659, the free burghers, who had gone to church, had seen a large gathering of Khoi across the Liesbeek River, where they were singing and shouting. It was hoped that such a good and effective watch was being kept that the raiders would not be able to get many of the cattle without sacrificing their men.

Building on previous successes, the Commander sought to extend the growth of vines. Many cuttings were handed out free of charge to the free burghers "who practically had to be forced to accept them." The Commander had ten to twelve thousand cuttings taken to a two morgen (about five acres) enlargement of the previous vineyard at Boscheuvel. Other fruit culture was also to be increased with thousands of orange, apple and lemon trees in the Commander's orchards.

The energetic Wouter Mostert, the miller and brick maker, was building a new water mill to replace the horse mill which could no longer be reliably used as a result of the theft of draught oxen, both the animals of the VOC and of the free burghers. Two months later, on 27 October 1659, the mill was in working order and ready to produce flour from the good wheat, rye and barley harvests. This had resulted in the garrison and labourers being given a monthly ration of forty pounds of freshly baked bread apart from their board money. Two cooks, who had become freemen, had set up a burghers' bakery.

In December, came the startling news that Harry, the former Khoi ringleader, had escaped from Robben Island at night in a small boat, which had so many leaks in it that it was said to be remarkable that it had remained afloat. The boat had been found in a creek at the Sand Sea, over a day's journey from the fort. but there had been no sign of Harry. The Commander was furious and sent a letter of reprimand to Rijk Overhagen, the supervisor on Robben Island, castigating him for being so imprudent as to let Harry escape in the first place.

Meanwhile, development and domestic innovations in the community continued. Building improvements were the subject of a report in January 1660, with praise for the newly-baked tiles. They were good for the roofing of the water mill and proof against fire from the outside, unlike thatched roofs, which were very easily set alight by external causes such as sparks flying from the chimney. There was general approval for replacing thatch on all VOC buildings, after the recent destruction by fire of Hendrik Boom's house had seriously interrupted his work as head gardener. Since Wouter Mostert's tiles were much in demand, he was instructed to make as many as he could; the size required was six inches wide and twelve inches long. It was agreed that the VOC would at its own cost convey the tiles by cart or wagon from the oven. There could be no clearer indication of the importance which the parsimonious VOC attached to the thatch replacement policy. Early in the following month, February 1660, the weather was at its summer best and the Commander took advantage of it by making a tour of inspection of the farms, both of the free burghers and of the VOC employees. He found everyone working well, ploughing the stubble and some were also beginning to thresh their new grain.

Towards the end of March, an alarming note was struck in the journal when it reported the unreliability of the VOC dependents and their desertion from ships. The Company's *Schapenjacht* was thus in great danger of being deserted by her crew at some time or other, since some of them were amongst the stowaways on the return fleet which had not long since left the Cape. Jan Reijnierssen of Amsterdam as a free burgher was appointed quartermaster in charge of the *Schapenjacht* after he had been ruined by the robberies of the Khoi and was now said to be destitute.

Early in April, peace was made with the Kaapmans, who were apparently delighted. An annual day of thanksgiving and prayer was to be observed. However, later in the month, the matter of defection was again a source of anxiety when the Council of Policy noted that no fewer than twenty Company servants and eighteen freemen were stowaways on a ship of the return fleet bound for Holland. Their remaining possessions at the Cape were confiscated by the VOC. Such a large number of discontents reflected both the physical difficulties of coping with the living conditions, the Khoi interventions and the general penny-pinching principle of the VOC policies. In a further entry in the journal, it was recorded that in the annual appointing of burgher councillors to the Council of Policy, Wouter Mostert was one of four appointed and he was to be the senior member since he had been a freeman for the longest time. It was noted that free farmers and burghers should always carry their firearms to prevent "tumults, disturbances, and hostile action on the part of the Aborigines." However, they were not often used.

Not infrequently, fickle winds upset the navigation of ships approaching or leaving Table Bay. In mid-May 1660, a French ship, *La Maréchal*, ran aground because of the strong north-west wind. It transpired that with her foresail set, she had sailed before the wind head on into the sand. Two notes were sent ashore in a barrel asking for help. The ship appeared to be well supplied with clergy and on the next day a bishop and three priests landed. The crew were requested to hand over their arms for security reasons but they were not keen to do this on the grounds that they would need them inland when searching for food. Indeed one of the officers became abusive and used language which displeased the Dutch. Since *La Maréchal* had a crew of one hundred and forty five men and the ship was breaking up, the Commander had the difficult task of arranging temporary accommodation for the French, and he was uncertain as to how they were likely to behave after a long voyage which had ended in shipwreck. It was decided that some might be employed by the VOC to assist in construction work, but the following Sunday in church a warning to beware of the French was read out after the sermon. "No-one shall permit or tolerate these men to conduct any religious ceremony other than according to the reformed faith while they are in this house or on this property."

It soon became apparent that the French had landed a great quantity of brandy from the ship and that they had offered it for sale to "sundry persons." The situation was eased somewhat when nearly half of the French were able to find places on a ship bound for Batavia, after a shipwrecked stay of five weeks at the Cape. However, not until March 1661 was the problem of sending home the French priests resolved, when a meeting of the Broad Council tackled the question of their repatriation. It was agreed that "the bishop, Monseigneur Estienne, and Monseigneur Fredijn shall travel in the *Malacca* and sit at the table in the Captain's room; and outside the Captain's room, the bishop's surgeon Frère Patte and his attendant named Fantasie." Other priests were distributed around four other ships. A year later, the hulk of *La Maréchal* burnt out.

Throughout van Riebeeck's final year in office at the Cape, his journal indicated that much time had been spent in tidying up and consolidating earlier progress.

On 13 May 1661, the Commander was occupied in marking out the hedge of wild bitter-almonds which they had begun to plant the previous year and which was growing well. It promised to grow into an exceptionally fine thick hedge in five or six years' time. This hedge was extended to include the Boscheuvel and Baerss rivers. During a heavy rainy season, the latter flowed into False Bay as well as Table Bay.

At the end of the month, the Commander made a tour of inspection during which he noted that many of the free burghers had to be spurred on in their farming. There was still a great deal of wheat to be sown, although in many fields it was already sprouting well. Van Riebeeck decided that his farm at Boscheuvel with its own crops, citrus orchards and vineyard was to be sold by him. He did not wish to plant anything more on the farm, since he intended leaving soon and thus wished to sell it with all trees and crops.

The Company's garden continued to thrive, and at the end of July van Riebeeck and his wife picked the first two lemons. Six weeks later, the men were busy in the gardens transplanting all the Dutch fruit trees and especially grafting quince on Dutch and Cape thorn trees, which looked promising. The same applied to the lemon trees, a few more of which were coming into bloom and promised more fruit than the previous year. In time, as their yield increased, they would provide excellent refreshment for passing ships. This would be of special significance in view of their high vitamin C content, the lack of which on board ship led as we have seen to scurvy and other diseases.

Another insight into life in the community was given in a Council report where the misdemeanours of a burgher councillor were recorded in a way that showed the importance attached to the figureheads in local government setting a suitable image. The 'free sawyer', Leendert Cornelissen of Zevenhuijse, a burgher councillor elected the previous year, instead of setting the freemen an honourable and dignified example, had daily been behaving in a more and more debauched manner by drinking, celebrating, brawling and swearing. He thus not only brought into disrepute his own character and the important office which he held but also tarnished "the lustre" of the Council, on which he had a seat when it considered abuses committed by free burghers and he had the right to cast a vote of censure. For these and several other reasons, as well as the desire to preserve the dignity and respect of the Council, it was resolved no longer to admit the said Leendert Cornelissen to the Council but to dismiss him from his office as burgher councillor.

From time to time in these early years, the difficult task of obtaining cattle from the Saldanhars and other tribes in the vicinity was complicated by disease. In November 1661, it was recorded that disease was rampant particularly among their livestock, some of which had died. Portions of the carcasses had been brought and sold to the Dutch everywhere on the pretence that the meat had been obtained from slaughtered animals. As a result, there was already much disease among the Dutch.

In contrast with the meat trade problems, the production of food from crops growing in the VOC's gardens invariably drew a more positive comment. At midsummer 1661, the journal reported: "The Dutch fruit trees are giving more and more promise of the success we wish for, especially the apples and quinces, which are developing well on a few young trees, of which there are as yet only three or four. Others are already in bloom and ought soon to be bearing fruit when they are somewhat older and become more firmly rooted. The greatest advantage of the fruit trees is that the fruit will be properly matured in time for the arrival of the return fleet and of other ships leaving the Fatherland in autumn and winter. We see that the lemon and orange trees are also promising, for some of them already have a fair crop. The vines are bearing exceptionally well and so is the olive tree, which bore last year; in fact its branches are weighted down to the ground. This month there were already a few ripe black currants and gooseberries. The cherries are now beginning to ripen. As the cherry trees grow older they may bear more fruit but these fruits will have to be consumed by the inhabitants because at that time there are few ships."

From time to time, the Council minutes recorded a marriage ceremony and one ceremony which took place on 26 January 1662 was typical.

"At close of the service last Sunday, the betrothed persons, Abraham Gabbema of the Hague, batchelor, and fiscal here, and Petronella Does of Doesburgh, spinster, had their third banns called according to Christian usage. No objections were raised and we find no reason why these two should not be allowed to proceed with the marriage. The Council has therefore decided, in accordance with the resolution of the 4th instant, to allow the solemnisation of matrimony to take place in the name of the Lord, and has therefore agreed, in order that everything may proceed legally and in due form, to the greater glory of God, that the Secretary of the Council should conduct the marriage in the absence of a parson, the marriage to take place publicly in open Council. Accordingly, after the reading of the sermon today the wedding duly and lawfully took place in public and in the name of the Lord."

In his journal, van Riebeeck often emphasized the settlers' growing curiosity about the rumoured terrain and peoples of the hinterland of the Cape. A number of expeditions had been arranged in the hope of finding the Namaqua people, who were believed to inhabit an area near what came to be recognised as the Oliphants River. Early in 1662, a party of twelve, led by Sergeant Pieter Everaerts had made such an attempt. However, they turned back on finding a stretch of country so barren and salty that it was impossible to traverse. The soil was as dry as a plank and there was nothing but sand dotted with molehills. There was neither foliage nor grass there, nothing but an occasional puddle of muddy water, so brackish that its edges were encrusted with white salt. These unsuitable conditions forced the explorers to turn back.

By this time, van Riebeeck's ten years at the Cape of Good Hope were drawing to a close, much to his relief. On 6 May 1662, the Hon. Zacharias Wagenaar was formally presented to all the people at the Fort as Commander and his Commission from their Honours the Governor-General and Councillors of India was read out by the secretary from the porch, whereupon His Honour was unanimously accepted and acknowledged as Commander in succession to the Hon. Jan van Riebeeck.

Jan van Riebeeck sailed from the Cape two days later on 8 May 1662 and arrived at Batavia on 6 July after a two month voyage. He and his family were housed in a rather ramshackle old Dutch house, without immediate prospects of further employment. In September, he was appointed to the Council of India as a reward for his services. This move was followed almost immediately by his appointment as Commander and President of the VOC settlement in Malacca, a rundown post which had seen more affluent days. Van Riebeeck was not impressed by this offer which was scarcely promotion.

Maria van Riebeeck, his wife, had continued to draw praise and acclaim. She was liberal-minded, tolerant in her opinions, hospitable and kindly-hearted. Her natural grace had been an asset as Governor's wife and she had been a great support to her husband through their fifteen years of married life. She had borne him eight children, four sons and four daughters. Five children had been born at the Cape and the four daughters were with her when she died at the early age of 35, at Malacca. When Secretary to the High Government of India in 1666, Jan van Riebeeck married Maria Scipio, a widow whose first husband had also been an officer of the VOC, in Sumatra. After ten years, his own health started to fail rapidly and he died in Batavia on 18 January 1677.

During the decade he had held command at the Cape, van Riebeeck had persisted energetically to develop the settlement, send expeditions to explore the interior, build up a seal fishery industry, explore the coast, extend the jetty to improve facilities for providing provisions for passing ships, and to expand the Company's cultivated land as far as Rondebosch, where he had built Groot Schur, a great storehouse. However, van Riebeeck had not been without his critics, who had felt he was temperamental, and this stood in the way of his promotion after leaving the Cape. Historians differ in their interpretation of his personality. One of the more objective opinions is that of the South African historian C.L. Leipoldt whose biography of van Riebeeck concluded with this summary:

"To the settlement that he founded and wisely governed for eleven years he was a prudent and perspicacious father, identifying himself with its interests for as long as he was able to do so. He found a barren foreshore and left a cultivated colony. He had faith and vision – faith in the future of his foundation, the vision of a white settlement at the southern extremity of Africa that would be a haven of civilisation in a barbaric land and another gem in the coronet of the Company. To him South Africa owes the beginnings of its industrial and agricultural activities. He believed that there were copper, silver and precious stones hidden somewhere in the mysterious hinterland, where lay the fabled Monomotapa and the marvellous realm of Prester John. To South Africa he must remain a figure wrapped in the romance that clings round the pioneer and that neither time nor misrepresentation can wholly dull."

CHAPTER 7

Lean Years of Weak Leadership

The contrast between van Riebeeck and his successor Zacharias Wagenaar could hardly have been greater. The lively energy which had characterised van Riebeeck's command and leadership of the growing Cape establishment was completely lacking in his successor. Impassive and dull, not to say indolent, Zacharias Wagenaar lacked any sense of ambition or drive for his post as Commander of the Cape, even though glad to accept the post for which he had applied.

He was born at Dresden on 9 May 1614, the original spelling of his name being Wagner. He had served with the Dutch West India Company for seven years from 1634 to 1641 in Dutch Brazil. His skill as an artist of fauna and flora had produced a remarkable 'Animal Book of Brazil.' Among his drawings of sea creatures was a curious looking flat fish known by its Indian name of gueperua, though to the Dutch it was better known as pig-fish, largely on account of its pig-like snout and indiscriminate eating habits.

Earlier in his career with the VOC, Wagenaar had been a man of greater energy and had held responsible posts in the East but at the expense of his health. Immediately before coming to the Cape, he had been a supervisor of buildings at Batavia but he had found the task "too burdensome for my gouty carcass." This self-description hardly seems an obvious recommendation for a Commander designate of the Cape. After his installation on 6 May 1662, he was confined to his house for weeks on end through ill-health, when routine administration was all he could manage. This had been an inauspicious beginning, but upon

FIGURE 5 Peixe Porco Gueperua or pig-fish drawn by Zacharias
Wagenaar in *Animal Book of Brazil 1640* as adapted in *Zacharias
Wagner, Second Commander of the Cape* by O.H. Spohr,
published by A.A. Balkema, Cape Town, 1967.

finding good relationships with the Khoi, the Commander sought to build on them by making an inland expedition to the Cochoqua tribe, with the intention of extending trade in cattle and sheep. Eva the Khoi accompanied the party as interpreter. However, the Commander found the eight-day expedition so disagreeable that he never went near the Khoi again. A man of strong faith in the Protestant tradition, Wagenaar had Eva baptised. She was later married, on 2 June 1664, to Pieter van Meerhof, the surgeon, after which a little marriage feast was given in the Commander's house. This union was notable for being the second mixed marriage between a European and a Khoi.

In September 1664, news reached the Cape from Europe that there was a likelihood of war between England and the Netherlands. The Council of Seventeen became anxious that the importance, both political and economic, of the Cape settlement would be endangered by a sudden armed attack from the sea. In the following June, 1665, Commander Wagenaar, received the most disturbing news that war had indeed broken out in Europe in March that year. This was the second Anglo-Dutch naval war, which ended in 1667 with the Treaty of Breda after the English docked fleet was defeated by the Dutch at Chatham. Commercial rivalry between the two nations and interpretation of Charles II's Navigation Acts of 1660 and 1663, which aimed to deal with the threat to British shipping by the rise of the Dutch maritime trade, had led to hostilities and war had been declared after the English had captured New Amsterdam (New York).

Thus the replacement of van Riebeeck's fort by something more substantial was decided on in 1665. After further deliberations, the Seventeen resolved to build a proper fortress of hewn stone, which would support large guns and be capable of housing a sizeable garrison. The arrival of Commissioner Isbrand Goske in August had heralded the choice of a site for the new castle. After an eight day tour of inspection, he had recommended a site 248 yards east of the earthen fort and this had been approved at a meeting of the Broad Council.

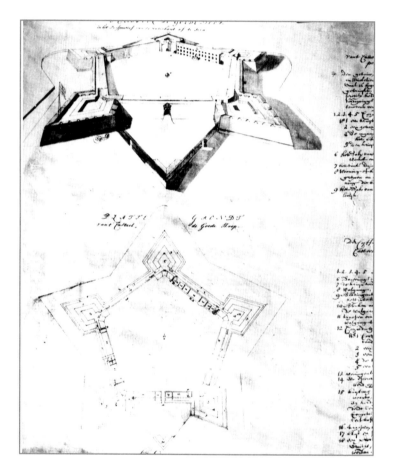

FIGURE 6 Plan of the Castle at the Cape of Good Hope.
(Reproduced by permission of the National Library
of South Africa).

The Council of Seventeen had sent instructions to the Commander to establish a workforce by keeping three hundred soldiers from passing ships to clear the site, get ready the materials, and start quarrying the stone from Signal Hill. The castle was designed by the engineer Pieter Dombaer, who was appointed to superintend the construction. The plan of the castle followed that widely used by Vauban in his work as military engineer to Louis XIV; it was in the shape of a pentagon with five bastions, with each bastion to be named after the titles of the Prince of Orange: Oranje, Nassau, Leerdam, Buuren, and Catzenellenbogen. The main entrance had originally faced on to the sea but it subsequently proved to be too open to storms and was moved to the west side in 1682 by a later Governor, Simon van der Stel.

Preparatory work for the building operations included the collecting of a party of convicts and slaves, who were detailed to gather shells from the shores of Robben Island for making lime mortar. For fuel to burn in the limekiln, timber had to be fetched, with difficulty, from Hout Bay (hout being the Dutch for wood). Small red bricks, typical of those still to be seen in the Netherlands, were imported for use in the construction of interior walls within the castle. As part of the exercise, all wagons that could be spared from agriculture were pressed into service for the transport of building materials. "The farmers were paid at the rate of six shillings and three pence per day for each wagon with oxen and one man, whether a hired servant or a slave."

After five months with this labour force at work, the site was sufficiently cleared for the Commander to lay the ceremonial foundation stone on 2 January 1666. This important occasion was a gala day and everyone came out dressed in their best clothes to take part in the celebrations. Farmers with their wives and children came in from Rondebosch and Wynberg. Company servants and other residents came from Table Valley and sailors came ashore from their ships. There were four ceremonial stones to be laid. Commander Wagenaar laid the first one, the clergyman

83

Johan van Arckel placed the second, the 'sekunde' (second in command at the fort) Abraham Gabbema laid the third, and the fourth stone was laid by the fiscal Hendrik Lacus. After the formal part of the ceremony had been concluded, a feast was prepared from two oxen, six sheep, one hundred large loaves of bread and eight casks of Cape ale. In the best Netherlands tradition, some lines of poetry specially written for the occasion were then read by the Commander.

Subsequently the speed with which the castle was built varied with the political news from Europe, where war continued to rage on land and at sea. At times when there appeared to be the possibility of an attack from France, work on the castle became more urgent. As the risk receded so the pace slowed. The castle was first occupied in 1674 by the Governor Isbrand Goske but it was not completed until 1679, when Simon van der Stel became the first commander to have the use of the whole building. Today, Cape Town Castle is the oldest surviving building in South Africa. Only two weeks after the stone laying ceremony, there was another gathering at the same place for the funeral of the clergyman Johan van Arckel. He had only just arrived at the Cape with Commissioner Isbrand Goske in the previous August 1665 and his appointment had been cut short by a brief illness. A few months later, Commander Wagenaar's wife also died and, like van Arckel, she was buried among the foundations of the new church within the Castle.

Commander Wagenaar was impatient with the obstructive attitude and uncooperative behaviour of a number of the early settlers. His report on the subject to the Seventeen included these comments: "There are not above six or eight farmers who are, either in repute or in fact, respectable and industrious men; the rest are depraved from their youth upwards, lazy, drunken fellows who care as little for their Dutch servants as for beasts." A later report from Wagenaar referred to the same problems when he recommended deportation to Mauritius, to which island he had already banished three families from Rondebosch.

Less than two years after his arrival at the Cape, Commander Wagenaar pleaded successfully with the Seventeen to let him go on the grounds of ill health. Cornelis van Quaelberg was announced as his successor but the handover could not be immediate. In the event, van Quaelberg, accompanied by his family, left Holland on 19 December 1665 in the *Dordrecht*. He had to contend with an appalling journey, eventually reaching the Cape on 20 August 1666. When the ship arrived there was not a single person in sound health on board. On the voyage, one hundred and ten sailors had died, and there was so much sickness that no furling of sail could be attempted without help from those ashore. So severe had been the storm in the North Sea that the *Dordrecht* had had to put into the Faroe Islands for shelter for nine weeks before attempting to proceed further. Van Quaelberg took office at the end of September and Zacharias Wagenaar left with his daughter-in-law on 1 October in a cleaned up *Dordrecht* bound for Batavia. An unsuspected philanthropist at heart, when he spent a month at the Cape in February 1668 on his way to Europe from Batavia, he gave a sum of money for the Church Council to use for the assistance of the poor. He died in Amsterdam on 1 October 1668.

Such hazards as had afflicted the voyage of the *Dordrecht* were not restricted to the outward bound fleet. Always unpredictable, at the mercy of the elements, one particular return voyage to be afflicted by considerable misfortune and severe problems was the return fleet of the same year, 1665. This fleet was known to be carrying a particularly diverse and valuable cargo. The Commander-in-Chief of the English Royal Navy, Lord Sandwich, had remarked: "I am apt to believe that scarce at any time in one place so great a mass of wealth was ever heaped together."

Consisting of thirteen ships, the fleet was the largest yet to be assembled at Batavia. Four of the vessels were Flute ships and the remaining nine were well-defended East Indiamen. The incredible cargoes consisted not only of hundreds of tons of spices, including cinnamon, mace, cloves, nutmeg, pepper, the dye indigo, and saltpetre for making gunpowder. There were also Eastern carpets and silks and a large collection of precious stones, said to have included three thousand diamonds, three thousand rubies and eighteen thousand pearls together with sixteen thousand pieces of fine China. The Vice-Admiral commanding the fleet was Jacob Borghorst, on his way home from his post as Commander of the VOC station at Colombo. Seeking to improve his personal fortunes, he wore a waistband containing eight pouches of precious stones, which he believed he could sell in Europe for about twelve thousand pounds sterling, a vast fortune at that time.

Leaving behind two follow-up ships to bring last-minute cargo and mail, the rest of the fleet sailed from Batavia on 24 December 1664. It was not long before their troubles started. After clearing Sunda Strait, off Java, a violent storm raged for five days and the crews became alarmed by the appearance of a large comet, which they saw as an ill omen. As the fleet approached Mauritius, a week of hurricanes occurred in the middle of February 1665, causing damage to the ships and the loss of eighty men. At the beginning of March more storms broke out and one ship was lost. The fleet rounded the Cape and anchored in Table Bay on 11 March and stayed for six weeks to rest after such an horrendous first part of the journey to Holland. The knowledge that England and the Netherlands were at war, and that there was a serious outbreak of plague on the Continent, did nothing to raise the spirits of the crews. While waiting at the Cape, the fleet was joined by the two following ships from Batavia.

The fleet of twelve ships finally sailed from the Cape on 22 April 1665, and among the passengers was the Company's gardener Hendrik Boom on his way home to the Netherlands. Severe storms on 9 July caused four ships to become detached from the rest of the fleet. Because of the war it was necessary for the fleet to avoid the English Channel and to pass round the north of Scotland. On 24 July, they ran into a bank of dense fog, which lasted for several days and when it cleared only six ships could be seen. More stormy weather was experienced in early August, by which time they were not far from the Arctic Circle, in the hope of avoiding the English fleet. They then found their colleagues hiding in Norwegian fjords. It was decided to sail on to the neutral port of Bergen where there were a number of other Dutch ships waiting to be rescued by the distinguished admiral and Dutch maritime leader, de Ruyter. First, however, Bergen harbour was blockaded by seventeen British warships. A decision was taken to defend the Dutch merchant ships. Seven of the largest Dutch East India Company ships were moved into the front line and a four hour battle ensued. The English were beaten off, with four hundred and fifty men killed; the Dutch losses were considerably lighter.

Within a few days, de Ruyter's well-armed ships arrived to escort the merchant fleet home but were subjected to an early blizzard on 9 September, which scattered ships all over the North Sea. Two of the most valuable ships from Borghorst's fleet, which had travelled further to the west than they had intended, were captured off the coast of Scotland. The Vice-Admiral and twelve hundred VOC sailors were taken prisoner and Admiral Borghorst lost all his precious stones. The Council of Seventeen had sent four ships to search for the missing ships from Batavia, some of which were in different North Sea ports. Ten were eventually accounted for but it was early 1666 before the last two reached home ports, the journey having taken more than twice the normal length of time.

Once installed as Commander at the Cape in September 1666, Cornelis van Quaelberg did not take long to show that he was an inward-looking, self-centred man. He had been in charge of the Company's factory at Masulipatnam from 1652 to 1657, but there was no evidence to suggest that this management post equipped him for the task of Commander of the Cape. It was presumed that the Council of Seventeen must have thought his qualifications and experience relevant for the Cape, but this never became apparent to the Cape residents. He displayed an irritating habit of belittling the work of his predecessor and publicising the assumption that his way of doing things was better.

Early in 1667, there was a surprise arrival at the Cape of a French fleet of twelve ships under the command of the Viceroy of French possessions in the East, Monsieur de Mondevergne. For some years, the Dutch had watched anxiously attempts by the French to establish an eastern trading pattern, and these developments now had the active support of Louis XIV. The Netherlands Government became substantially more alarmed when it became apparent that an able officer of long experience with the VOC had turned his allegiance to the French cause. Of French descent, Pierre Caron had long held responsible posts at the VOC head-quarters in Batavia. He had offered his services to Colbert, the French Minister of Finance, Industry and Commerce and, in due course, Caron had set up the first French factory on the coast of Hindustan (India).

The French fleet had put into Table Bay because the voyage from La Rochelle to Madagascar had been seriously mismanaged. At their first port of call, Pernambuco in Brazil, it had been necessary to stock up on stores owing to wastage. A Dutch sailor, who had been there at the time, wrote a report to the Seventeen about the state of the Admiral's ship. He described it as so filthy that it would be a wonder if pestilence did not break out, and so ill-provided with everything requisite that he did not believe she could ever reach Madagascar.

On arrival at Table Bay, the Viceroy, Monsieur de Mondevergne, had saluted with five guns and the port had replied, as was the custom, with three guns. Commander van Quaelberg sent a message on board to invite the French Viceroy to come ashore. The invitation was declined, so the Commander himself went on board to call. He offered the Viceroy any supplies that he might need. This offer was accepted with enthusiasm, and the VOC stores were virtually stripped. In addition, much skilled labour was placed at the disposal of the French visitors, to repair one of their ships which was leaking dangerously. It was surprising that the Commander had been so generous to the French fleet in view of the underlying political tension. Displaying a certain naiveté, van Quaelberg had written a report on the French visit to the Seventeen, which reached them months later in November 1667. So serious was the unanimous disapproval of the Directors that they wrote van Quaelberg a letter dismissing him from the Company's service. He could go either to Batavia or back to Holland and he was instructed to hand over his responsibilities to Jacob Borghorst, who would succeed him.

Jacob Borghorst duly arrived from Holland on 16 June 1668 in typical ill health. He remained an invalid and for most of the time of his command the administration of the Cape was carried on by his colleagues on the Council of Policy. One of the group, the 'secunde' Hendrik Lacus, had fallen from grace and was under suspension for misappropriation of stores under his care. The responsibilities of government fell on the fiscal Cornelis de Cretzer, who was well able to cope in the calm circumstances prevailing, with only the cattle trade and the Company's gardens calling for any kind of overseeing.

Explorations were made from time to time and a greater knowledge of areas further away from the Cape settlement was building up. The coast had been well charted northwards beyond the mouth of the Oliphants River, and in an easterly direction as far as Mossel Bay. Inland, the Berg River had been followed from its source to the sea and the attractive Tulbagh Basin in the far north-eastern corner of the south-western Cape lowlands had been visited by Europeans, as had the Breede River Valley. The Tulbagh Basin presented a dramatic sight, being a depression at the head of a high valley, with a water system of its own. The grassy valley of the Upper Breede, six or seven miles wide, was enclosed on each side by a formidable rocky barrier. Beliefs that there was mineral wealth in the vicinity of the Cape was finally investigated in 1669 by a party of miners from Europe. Their search for metals had taken them in particular to Table Valley, the Paarl Mountain and to Riebeeck's Kasteel. Over a period of years, excavations had been made in various parts of the country but nothing had been found.

An important visitor in 1670 was the Commissioner Mattheus van der Broeck. He arrived while he was acting as Admiral to the homeward bound fleet of richly laden ships from Batavia. An able senior employee of the VOC, he gave the Commander a list of questions to answer, including a question about the production of grain. It had long been a concern of the Seventeen that the Cape was not yet self-sufficient in wheat. The regular need for imported rice from Batavia was a cost which the Directors were most anxious to eliminate. Resulting from Commissioner van der Broeck's investigations, Commander Borghorst decided to use land known as Hottentots Holland, an area inland and easterly from the Cape, recognised by the Khoi to be the choicest portion of the whole country for grain farming. He had once been there and it had occurred to him that it would be a good area to cultivate, and it later proved fertile and well suited to the growing of wheat and cattle pasture.

Commander Borghorst had continued to suffer ill-health and was asking to be relieved of his post within a few months of his arrival. The Directors instructed that the Company's merchant Jan van Aelmonden should be detained from the next return fleet on which he had been expected to be a passenger. The fleet duly arrived but there was no sign of van Aelmonden. In his place, the Seventeen chose another of their ageing servants with broken health after years in the East, Pieter Hackius. As was the case with so many of the Cape Commanders who came and went in the thirteen years between the retirement of Jan van Riebeeck and the appointment of Simon van der Stel, Pieter Hackius arrived in poor health. Indeed, he was so unwell that three months elapsed after his arrival before he was able to take his first Council meeting. One of the first matters requiring attention was the increasing danger of lions and leopards attacking the Company's herds and flocks in the settlement. It was decided that the reward for killing a lion in the near vicinity of the settled areas was to be increased to six pounds five shillings.

When a second large fleet from France, this time on its way to the East, approached Table Bay its Commander, Admiral de la Haye, politely fired a five-gun salute and received one in reply. The Admiral, who regarded this response as an insult to the French throne, did not behave in the manner of an exemplary visitor. Six of his ships put into Saldanha Bay where they laid claim to the Dutch station and made prisoners of the small group of Dutch soldiers there under sergeant Hieronymus Cruse. They also captured some Dutch fishermen, who were going about their normal business in the bay. The VOC flag was taken down and the French flag hoisted in its place.

Against these events, the Council of Policy lodged a strong protest, and Commander Hackius resolutely refused to equip the French fleet with any stores or provisions from the Company's possessions, remembering what had happened four years previously. The French Admiral was, however, told that he might buy vegetables from any of the farmers who had a quantity available. Before sailing on, the French fleet released their Dutch prisoners and left no garrison behind. Some four months later, the Dutch garrison was strengthened by three hundred men and normality was restored to operations at Saldanha Bay.

In February 1671, the Commissioner Isbrand Goske made a second visit to the Cape settlement. On this occasion, he sought to introduce legislation related to slaves. Like van Riebeeck before him, he was concerned that slaves were heathen and "he found it desirable" that they should be instructed in the Christian faith as revealed by the Dutch Reformed Church. The slaves were to

attend church twice on Sundays and to receive religious instruction each evening. When they knew enough to profess a belief in
Christianity they could be baptised and married. It was already a
custom that slave children should go to school "so that none
might grow up heathens."

Commander Hackius became increasingly an invalid, and was not
able to undertake the entertaining of senior officers from ships at
anchor in the bay. This task sometimes fell to the 'secunde'
Cornelis de Cretzer, who had for some time been the most
responsible and efficient member of the Cape administration.
Unfortunately, at a dinner party where he was the host, de
Cretzer lost his temper with two of his guests. One was the captain of a ship and the other a passenger on the same vessel, who
were engaged in such a row at the dinner table that the passenger
was attacked. Unable to pacify them, de Cretzer stabbed the captain with his rapier. Filled with remorse for the error of a moment,
de Cretzer fled into hiding. No-one wanted to see him prosecut-
ed so he was able to slip away quietly on a ship to Amsterdam.
After investigating the case, the Directors pronounced him
blameless and restored him as secunde (deputy) at the Cape, a
post where he had been both efficient and popular. However, the
hand of fate decided otherwise. In the course of his journey back
to the Cape, his ship was attacked by a Moorish vessel and the last
report about de Cretzer indicated that he had been sold on the
slave market in Algiers, a surprising misfortune for a man of intelligence and initiative.

Meanwhile, the administration of the Cape was virtually at a
standstill. For reasons attributed to his health, or the lack of it,
Commander Hackius seldom stirred and the three important
posts under him had all been held by the unfortunate de Cretzer
to whom there was no obvious successor. There were two able
men at the Cape, but they were both in lowly positions without
any experience of leadership in administration. One of them was
Hendrik Crudop, a young man more cultivated than many who

had progressed in the service of the Company and he was secretary to the Council. The other figure was the sergeant, Hieronymus Cruse, a man of practical ability but not of education.

He had gained valuable knowledge of the Cape and its hinterland as a leading explorer and he had a good understanding of the Khoi groupings. Although they would be consulted in areas where their expertise was of value to Council deliberations, neither of them had voting power. After months of deteriorating health, Commander Hackius died in office on 30 November 1671, and was buried within the new castle walls. Since no one individual was judged to have sufficient experience to assume temporary command of the Cape administration on their own, the government was run on a committee basis for several uneventful months.

The darkening political scene in Europe brought anxiety concerning the unfinished state of the castle. Louis XIV's aggression towards the Dutch provinces and his success in buying off England and Sweden led to the Netherlands being invaded by France on land and attacked by England at sea between 1672 and 1674. Work on the castle, which had been suspended for some time, was now to be tackled with renewed vigour and the garrison was to be enlarged. Woodwork for different parts of the castle buildings was being prepared in Amsterdam for shipment. Other construction material including bricks and tiles were also being sent out to augment those made at the Cape, and skilled artisans came in the same ship to do the work. To re-establish a competent administration for the Cape, three office holders were appointed from Amsterdam, Isbrand Goske as Commander, Albert van Breugel as secunde and Pieter de Neyn as fiscal.

The burden of replenishing the fleets, which fell on the VOC employees at the Cape, may be judged by some ten-year statistics. Between 1 January 1662 and 31 December 1671, three hundred and seventy VOC ships had called at Table Bay on their way to or from Holland. In addition, twenty-six French, nine English and two Danish ships also called. As a rule, each vessel would carry around one hundred and eighty men but a first class Indiaman would carry between three and four hundred crew. At that time, it required seventy or eighty men to hoist the huge mainsail of an Indiaman. Defence against possible attack by pirates was an additional reason for carrying a large crew. Experience had shown that at least one-third of the ship's company could be laid low by scurvy on a voyage that took longer than four months.

The total number of people who passed annually through the Cape was estimated to exceed seven thousand. It was quite usual for ships to pause for ten or twelve days during which time their crews would be consuming fresh provisions from the Company's gardens and meat from trade with the Khoi. The annual amount of meat consumed by the VOC ships and supplied at the Cape was estimated at three hundred and fifty cattle together with nearly four thousand sheep.

CHAPTER 8

Consolidation under
Two Governors

By the early 1670s, the Europeans felt themselves to be increasingly secure at the Cape. They had for their protection a garrison of three hundred men in Table Valley and a militia of one hundred burghers, some of them mounted on Javanese ponies. Attitudes towards the Khoi, who periodically came to graze their stock on the natural pastures of the south-western Cape, were tolerant unless and until the Europeans believed thefts of animals were taking place. When caught, punishment of the thieves was cruel but not out of line with the philosophy of the times. On one occasion, five men from a group of the Colchoquas led by Gonnema had been caught red-handed sheep stealing, and they had assaulted the herdsmen. They were bound and taken to the fort, where, despite many offers of cattle as ransom, they were tried and sentenced to flogging. Three, who were found guilty of assault, were branded and banished to Robben Island for fifteen years, the other two for seven years, to collect shells for the public good in return for food. In due course, all escaped from the island by boat.

The new 'secunde' (deputy), van Breugel, arrived in March 1672 from Holland on the *Macassar*. The councillors had gone on board to greet him and help him ashore. Unfortunately, while they were on board, a sudden south-easter sprang up, as is its wont in the month of March, and the party was kept on the *Macassar* for two days before they could reach the shore. Van Breugel was authorised to act as Commander in the absence of anyone more senior, and he took over immediately. Almost at the same time, part of the return fleet arrived bringing Admiral Arnout van Overbeke as Commissioner to the Cape. Having made an inspection of the settlement, the Commissioner believed it would make for greater stability in relationships with the different Khoi groups if a formal purchase of land from them were to be made. The Chief, to whom the Dutch had given the name 'Schacher', was the son of the chief, Fat Captain Congosoa, who had been the principal figurehead in van Riebeeck's time. The Commissioner found the chief willing to agree to the proposed land deal because he was shrewd enough to see that he would lose no more land than he had already lost. It was an odd transaction with strange values that did not mean very much to either party.

Exactly seven months after the arrival of van Breugel, the new Commander arrived. Isbrand Goske landed from the *Zuid Polsbroeck* on 2 October 1672, after a voyage of five months from Holland. By virtue of his rank, Isbrand Goske, Councillor Extraordinary of India, was styled Governor of the Cape, where he was installed on 2 October. He served for three and a half years at a politically sensitive time for the Dutch when they were engaged in an unequal struggle with most of the rest of Europe ranged against them, both on land and at sea. Goske was sent to the Cape by the Council of Seventeen at a time when an attack on the settlement might well have been expected. He had a sense of initiative and was the only Commander to make an impact on the Cape community between the rule of Jan van Riebeeck and that of Simon van der Stel.

Isbrand Goske's first task was to galvanise the workforce into a speedier completion of the castle. He was authorised to add to the number of workers by taking men from passing ships, but was faced with the difficulty that fewer ships were on the move because of the dangers in Europe, and no ships appeared to carry a full complement of crew. Even so, he found it possible to direct between two hundred and fifty and three hundred men to work

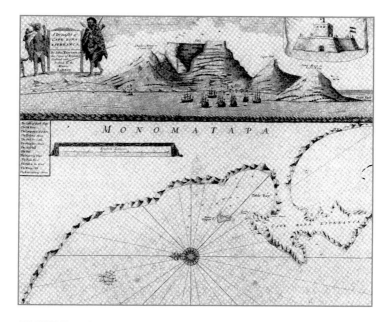

FIGURE 7   Table Bay From the *English Pilot*, originally published by John Seller 1670-71. Thornton Edition c.1703. Shows inset with the fort and a Khoikhoi family (South Africa Panorama 1960).

on the castle. As a short-term measure, the Governor had decided it would be prudent to bring van Riebeeck's earthen fort back into some semblance of practical use. He likened its appearance to a "ruined molehill."

Owing to the indisposition of Commander Hackius, nothing had been done to create a farming community at Hottentots Holland. It was nearly three years since Commander van der Broeck had authorised this. It was now more urgently required, as a bolt-hole for the garrison and for the castle in the event of the Cape settlement being attacked and possibly laid to waste. On 18 October 1672, sergeant burgher Cruythof led a construction party of twelve to start putting up buildings at Hottentots Holland, near the north-east corner of False Bay. The soil was rich and the fierce south-easters blew less strongly than they did at the Cape itself and they would thus be less of a hazard to the farmers.

At the start of Governor Goske's rule in 1672, the European population of the Cape was still small and it was remarkable that they had achieved so much. They numbered sixty four burghers, of whom thirty nine were married, sixty five children, and fifty three Dutch men servants. In addition, there were around three hundred and seventy VOC employees and soldiers. For some years, it had been difficult to tempt more settlers from Holland, where life was prosperous and employment good. The VOC was correctly seen as a miserly employer and a tough taskmaster, which looked on its eastern cargoes as being less expendable than the crews who brought them.

By the middle of 1674, work on the castle had reached the stage where it offered a better defence than did the old fort and the time had come for the garrison to move in. Then on 13 July, a dispatch ship bedecked with flags arrived in Table Bay with the news of Holland's peace with England by the Treaty of Westminster, which had been signed in February. From 1674 to 1678, the French were left with Sweden as their only effective ally, although making steady advances in the southern Netherlands and along the Rhine. Work on the castle could now proceed at a less hectic pace with a smaller labour force. The Governor's official residence within the castle started to be built in August 1674, on the outer side of the transverse wall dividing the castle into an outer and an inner courtyard. Simon van der Stel was the first governor to occupy the whole of the new premises and his fine council chamber and hall still remain an important feature of the Governor's lodging, otherwise considerably altered at a later date.

During the administration of Commander Goske, there was an important development in relations with the Khoi. In their trading with the Khoi for supplies of meat, the Dutch invariably brought copper, tobacco and beads to their side of the barter. In the mid-1670s, with more than twenty years experience behind them, the Director in Amsterdam believed that parties of Khoi would approach the Cape with cattle if they were short of the barter goods they desired. When this had proved not to be the case, it had been decided to send a trading party to the kraal of the Chief of the Chainouquas, Captain Dorha, better known to the Dutch as Captain Klaas. He himself had indicated a wish to trade and this new contact opened up a long period of agreeable involvement between 'Captain Klaas' and the VOC. At this time, there was a second Chainouqua clan led by 'Captain Koopman'. Both men were regarded as rulers by the Cape administration, and by way of recognition the captains were given staffs bearing the Company's arms engraved on brass heads, which became an award coveted by other leading tribesmen. Captain Klaas proved to be a firm supporter of the Dutch government at the Cape. An early example was the manner in which he responded to an unusual request for fifty young oxen suitable for moving stone blocks to the castle. In less than two weeks he had them ready.

In July 1675 came the death of Eva, the first baptised Khoi, who had been largely brought up in the household of Maria van Riebeeck as a competent domestic servant. She had readily learned the Dutch language and was on many occasions valuable as an interpreter between the Khoi and the Dutch. She had married van Meerhof, the surgeon, in one of the first mixed marriages of the Dutch settlement. However, after her husband's death, the Dutch had found that she had fallen into bad ways of behaving, deemed to be scandalous, including drunkenness and other misconduct, even living in a Khoi kraal from time to time. Banned to Robben Island for penitence, she had been allowed to return to Table Valley on the promise of better conduct. Her resolutions did not last and she died on Robben Island. However, the Governor decided that she should have a Christian funeral and be buried in the church at the castle.

A concern of Goske's administration had been the plight of children who became orphaned and destitute. The church assumed responsibility for their maintenance and a fund had been raised for the purpose. In 1674, its value exceeded one thousand pounds sterling, a considerable sum at the time. Together with interest of six percent the fund was enough to meet the demands made on it. Another organisation was set up the following year on the authority of the Council of Seventeen in a letter dated 28 September, known as the Orphan Chamber. Its need had become apparent when a number of widows remarried without ensuring that the children received their rightful share of the deceased parent's estate. It was not an offshoot of the Council of Policy, but a separate body with legal status. There was an enactment that "in future, no marriage of a widower or widow, whether a servant of the Company or a burgher, could take place in the colony without a certificate being first obtained from the Orphan Chamber that the rights of the children by the previous marriage were secured."

Early in 1676, the return fleet arrived in Table Bay. It was under the command of Nicholas Verburg, a senior employee of the Company, second only to the Governor General of the Indies, who produced a document which empowered him to make the usual inspection of a Commissioner. It so happened that Governor Goske had stipulated that he would have no Commissioner overseeing his work while he was in charge at the Cape. When it came to the point, however, he raised no objection to Verburg's inspection and used the Commissioner's report as notes of guidance for his successor.

Commissioner Verburg made no particular contribution to the affairs of the Cape but he did receive a petition from three of the burgher councillors acting on behalf of all the freemen. The petition had five requests: first, that some cattle, which had been taken from the Khoi, should be given to them outright rather than on loan. Second, that they be permitted to sell grain, fruit and

FIGURE 8 Young Khoisan girl and Dutchman
(Reproduced by permission of the National Library
of South Africa).

wine on an open market and at the best price that could be obtained, while paying legitimate taxes. Third, that they be allowed similar trading rights in commerce as were already common to freemen in Batavia. Fourth, that those among them without land should be assigned freehold farms at Hottentots Holland and be granted cattle on lease. Last, to help the poor, the cost of rice sold from the Company's stores should be reduced. Already, it would seem that an under-privileged section of the community was emerging.

Commissioner Verburg had felt unable to make any snap decisions and had passed the questions to the Seventeen in Amsterdam. In due course, a reply came back in which the first request was fully granted, the next three were partially granted and the last was refused. It was not the first time that the Directors' irritation had been aroused by reference to the import of rice from the East. They wanted increased production of wheat at the Cape to replace the import of rice as soon as possible. Any reduction in the price of rice would increase its demand which they were extremely anxious to avoid.

The administration of Isbrand Goske had been competent but unremarkable in other ways. He had kept the Company's gardens in order with slave labour. In order to free a dozen men to help on the castle, he had arranged to lease the garden and vineyard at Rustenburg to free men. Having a taste for oysters, he experimented in moving some from the warmer waters off the southern coasts to the more accessible shores of Table Bay, but his attempts came to nothing. With peace restored with England, the rival naval power, it was no longer thought necessary to retain the services of so senior a man as Isbrand Goske. A special agreement had been signed on 28 March 1674, under which the Dutch and English East India companies undertook to honour the aims of one another. Only the English East India Company had the size and ability to frustrate the trading of the Dutch.

The Council of Seventeen in November 1676 appointed Commander Johan Bax in place of Isbrand Goske, bringing him from Ceylon, where he was second in command. Although at the time of Governor Goske's departure from South Africa there was still war between the Dutch and the French, any fear of an attack on the Cape had receded and it was no longer necessary to look on employment of all spare hands at the castle as a matter of urgency. There were, however, attempts to involve part time labour in deepening the moat. On 25 November 1677, the Governor himself, his wife, his little son, all the Company's officers and their wives, the burgher councillors and other leading inhabitants with their wives, set to work for a considerable time carrying earth. The Governor carried out twelve baskets full and his wife six. After this, a regulation was made that everyone who passed the castle, male or female, irrespective of rank, should contribute to the same extent.

Progress in improving life in the community continued. Three years after setting up the Orphan Chamber in 1673, the Council of Policy created a Matrimonial Court consisting of four members, two of them Company servants and two burghers. All those who were intending to marry had to appear before this court to show that they were legally free to do so. Although not explicit, the implication was that irregular liaisons were not unknown and that the Council had felt morally obliged to try to do something about it. An important development took place early in 1678 when two farmers, Jochum Marquaart and Hendrik Elberts, leased from the Cape Government some of the land at Hottentots Holland for the purpose of grazing cattle and sheep. They were thus the first European settlers in South Africa to move beyond the settlement at the Cape. A month later, in February, they were followed by Henning Huising and Nicholas Gerrits, who set up as sheep farmers. In August of the same year, a fifth freeman, Cornelis Botma, also settled there as a sheep farmer. Of this group, Henning Huising became an important figure of whom more would be heard.

It continued to be difficult to attract settlers from the Netherlands, but there were five families who came out during the time of Johan Bax. Farmers were the category most needed but not many of the VOC servants had proved to be good at the work. It was the Company's policy to maintain a disciplined regime and any "worthless characters" would be given up to two warnings, and, if they were still unheeded, the individual would be deported by ship. Unlike a number of his predecessors, Johan Bax had, on the whole, enjoyed good health. Even so, he had developed a severe respiratory infection in the winter of 1678 and the following summer, after being confined to his bed for fifteen days, he died on 29 June. However, he had been able to appoint the 'secunde' (deputy) Hendrik Crudop as acting Commander and to inform the Council of Seventeen that he had done so. Welcome news from Europe came in February 1679 of peace between France and the Netherlands. Such a development led once again to a reduction in the workforce on the castle where virtually the only part still incomplete was the moat. On 29 April, the five bastions of the castle were duly named by the Council. The south point was named Oranje, the south-east Nassau, the east Catzenellenbogen, the north Buuren and the west Leerdam.

Meanwhile, the community at the Cape became more settled. The burgher Henning Huising was already making a success of his sheep grazing and was allowed to expand along the East River, with the proviso that he did not impinge on the Khoi who grazed their stock there. Two more burghers were keen to extend their farming operations: Pieter Visagie and Jan Mostert were permitted to work ground east of the Tigerberg, which was a haymaking area for fodder for the Company's stock, in the direction of what is now the town of Paarl.

A census taken in April 1679 listed the following population: eighty seven freemen, fifty five women, one hundred and seventeen children, thirty European men servants, one hundred and thirty three men slaves, thirty eight women slaves and twenty slave children, all in the settlement.

In place of Governor Bax, the Council of Seventeen, who had thought it unnecessary to maintain the post at governor level, decided to revert to a commander. Their choice fell upon one who was living in Amsterdam and working for the Amsterdam Chamber. He was very willing to fill the post, which would bring him promotion in the service of the Company, and he arrived in Table Bay on 12 October 1679. Welcomed by the secunde and the Council amid saluting cannons, he landed and was received by the garrison. No one in Holland nor in the Cape would have been aware that here was the most remarkable and outstanding leader in the development of Dutch South Africa, Simon van der Stel.

CHAPTER 9

Impact of Simon van der Stel

After the procession of infirm and unimaginative commanders under whom only slow progress was made at the Cape community, a marked change took place in 1679 with the appointment of Simon van der Stel.

The new Commander had powers of leadership and initiative, which heralded a new era in the growth and development of the Cape settlement and activity. He was born in 1639, in Mauritius, where his father had been Commander of the VOC station. Subsequently, his father had been decapitated in 1646 during an uprising in Ceylon. His mother had returned to Batavia where she died in 1652.

Her mother was Indian, and had van der Stel lived in the Cape during the apartheid era he would have been classed as Coloured. Through his father, he was connected with a leading family in Amsterdam where he was a much respected burgher. His employment with the VOC was not lucrative and he saw the opportunity for improvement in his promotion to the Cape.

The wife of the new Commander, Jacoba Six, had remained in Amsterdam and she never saw her husband again after his departure for South Africa. We are told that he continued to regard her with affection but there is some evidence that their relationship was overshadowed by 'libel', which meant some charge or legal proceedings. All his six children accompanied him to the Cape, including a two year old daughter, Catelina. His wife's sister Cornelia was among the family group, possibly in order to look after her niece, and remained at the Cape until her death in 1681. Of Simon van der Stel's sons, the eldest, Willem Adriaan, was to succeed him as Governor in 1681, his second son became a farmer at the Cape and the others moved on from South Africa in the service of the VOC, one of them to become Governor of Amboina.

In appearance, Simon van der Stel was regarded as "small with a dark complexion but an open cheerful countenance." He was a man of taste, who appreciated civilised surroundings. Shrewd and witty, he was a convivial host who soon became noted for his hospitality at his lodgings in the castle. He was both a good raconteur and a good listener. A passionate Dutchman at heart and a guardian of the Dutch language and customs, he attached great importance to the preservation of his country's culture at the Cape. In his eyes, everything Dutch was good and everything that was not Dutch was less good. It was not surprising that in later years his house at Groot Constantia should have been the first to be built in the emerging Cape Dutch style, although this was not the homestead we see now. It was an earlier form of a Dutch step gabled house, a forerunner of the style familiar to us today as Cape Dutch architecture.

Before Simon van der Stel took over the Cape administration, his predecessor acting Commander Crudop had introduced an important economic policy, which maintained its good effect throughout the new Commander's years in office. It concerned the trading in crops and merchandise whose franchises had been put up for auction, with the highest bidder being awarded sole rights of sale and distribution. Imported wines and spirits were the first goods to be handled in this way and, since it proved to be a good method of trading, brick making, tile making and grain milling soon followed. A reliable meat supply had been a problem but Henning Huising, who had settled in Hottentots Holland, was a dependable purveyor since he and a colleague had been in the meat trade since 1678. Van der Stel had given them a monopoly for three years to see how it developed. They had to supply wholesale meat to the garrison and to the public twice a week at the Company's fixed price. Other products, including Cape wines, were added to this system later.

By the time Simon van der Stel took over the command of the Cape settlement, it had become the most important calling point for revictualling on the shipping route between Europe and the East Indies. By his skill and enthusiastic leadership, he built up the trading station into a broader based community of increasing diversity in farming and expanding economic activity. By the end of his reign, the scene was set for the growth of cattle farming in particular and the evolution of the first 'Trekboers' (wandering farmers) or Afrikaners whose descendants were to have such a profound influence on the political history of South Africa.

Simon van der Stel was a man of vision, who saw the developing Cape settlement not as merely a trading station but as an extension of Holland overseas. He could make good use of the Council of Seventeen's recent decision to permit free immigrants from Europe and encourage the further growth of farming and commerce. By the end of his reign in 1699, a new generation was growing up and keen to break out of the south-western Cape. They wanted to push the frontiers of farming and settlement over new territory further east. All this, however, was in marked contrast to the pattern of settlement in the Cape that he had found on his arrival in 1679. At that time the castle on the shores of Table Bay and the Company's gardens, a little up the slope towards Table Mountain, dominated the scene. Nearby, inland from Table Bay along the banks of the Liesbeek River, were the majority of the farms of the free burghers. In the distance on the opposite side of False Bay, beneath the blue haze of the Hottentots Holland mountains, were the outlying VOC cattle stations. Beneath these mountains flowed the Eerste River in a fertile landscape which immediately attracted the new Commander's attention.

Van der Stel had spent his first few days acquainting himself with the castle and its immediate vicinity, including the Company's gardens blossoming in the spring sunshine. He then made his expedition to Hottentots Holland across the infertile Cape Flats to inspect the cattle stations, which he had found in good order. From here the Commander and his party of soldiers and servants turned northwards, and in an attractive grass covered landscape they came to the Eerste River whose divided channels enclosed a large wooded island, described as being "of great beauty." The party had spent a night there and the Commander readily saw that such agreeable surroundings would make a desirable place to live and farm. He named the spot Stellenbosch, which was to become the second European settlement in South Africa after Cape Town.

Settlers were not long in coming to this fertile and well-watered area. The first family arrived before the end of 1679; eight more moved in May 1680. The offer of as much land as could be managed and the freedom to select its position were practical inducements. Only tobacco was a forbidden crop; a farmer was allowed to grow anything else he might choose. As with all land owned or claimed by the VOC, a tithe was payable on produce grown in excess of that which the farmer and his family could consume themselves. Several more families moved to the Stellenbosch valley in 1681, which was a very good year for wheat growing. A number of the early farmers from the Liesbeeck River moved over to the wider spaces of Stellenbosch. For the first time, both the garrison and the burghers could be supplied with a quantity of wheat flour from which several months' supplies of bread could be made. The following year, 1682, brought a very different harvest after swarms of insects had attacked the crops. This infestation was repeated with lessening severity for several years before dying out altogether.

By 1683 thirty burgher families were installed at Stellenbosch. In recognition of the establishment of Stellenbosch, the Commander had been quick to recognise the civic value of setting up a petty court for the settling of local disputes between inhabitants. Civil litigation could be dealt with by the 'landdrost' or district magistrate in Stellenbosch unless it needed to be transferred to the larger court in Cape Town. The new court, however, of 'heemraad' or local administration, in the hands of four free burghers, was to be overseen by the Council of Policy in Cape Town to which the names of possible members were submitted for approval. Of the four original members, two retired at the end of 1683 and two at the end of 1684, which meant continuity was kept between the appointment and retiring of members. The responsibilities of this local court included the maintenance and development of local roads and the water supply. This represented a successful launching of decentralised local government in South Africa.

In September 1683, the first school was set up in Stellenbosch, the Commander having readily approved the idea. By a petition to the Council of Policy, the burghers had drawn attention to the presence of some thirty farmers, many of whom had families "but as yet there was no school in which the children could be taught the principles of Christianity as well as to read and write, so that the young were in danger of growing up as barbarians." It was also pointed out that the inhabitants of Stellenbosch were too far from the castle at Cape Town to be present at Sunday worship "and were thus liable to fall into careless habits." They had asked for the appointment of someone suitable to run the school, to read a sermon on Sundays and to visit those who were sick. The petition was well received by the Council of Policy; masons and carpenters were dispatched to build a house for the teacher, which was to include a large hall for use as a schoolroom. The first teacher to be appointed was Sybrand Mankadan and the school opened for its first pupils before the end of 1683.

The Commander had always taken a special interest in the affairs of Stellenbosch and the well-being of the people, which he regarded as very much his own creation. He liked to spend his birthday there in October and the occasion was made a public holiday for the inhabitants, who would dress in their best clothes and came to toast his health. Whenever possible, the Commander would arrive a few days early so as to be able to acquaint himself with local events and progress. The school children would form a procession behind their teacher, Sybrand Mankadan, carrying a banner which the Commander had given them. The school curriculum included boys over the age of nine having a weekly lesson in the use of arms, which was the beginnings of a young cadet force. The general teaching of the school included the rudiments of reading, writing and arithmetic, with much time devoted to the study of religious knowledge and there was an annual prize-giving at Christmas for the three most successful pupils.

The birthday celebrations in 1686 were enlarged into a Dutch fair or 'kermis' which occupied the first fortnight of October, culminating in the Commander's birthday on the last day. The fair took the form of a relaxed holiday event, and people would drive out from Cape Town in their wagons to enjoy a reunion with families and friends. During the fair, there were no restrictions on trading and everyone could buy and sell local produce as much as they liked. Among the colourful events which took place was the drilling of the militia and target practice. The target resembled a parrot or 'papegaai' which was fixed upon a pole in the centre of a circle with a radius of sixty feet. The marksmen chose their position in the order in which they had paid their subscription fees, which to residents of Stellenbosch were one shilling and to all others four shillings. They fired in the same order, standing and without rests for their guns. There were small prizes: for knocking off the head, four shillings; the right wing, two shillings; and the left wing, one shilling and six pence; the tail, one shilling; and a splinter, six pence. The grand prize was given to the one who succeeded in knocking off the rump and by so doing destroyed the whole figure. It amounted to five pounds in cash from the Company and with whatever subscription money was in hand, it had the advantage of showing the Company making a financial contribution to a popular event, a much needed boost to its image. The winner was escorted home in state by the whole body of shooters, and was given the title of 'King of the Marksmen' until someone could wrest it from him.

As we have seen, it was customary for leading figures of the VOC on instructions from the Council of Seventeen to arrive at the Cape as visiting Commissioners to inspect all aspects of life of the developing community. During the regime of Simon van der Stel, several dignitaries visited the Cape. In February 1682, the homeward bound fleet arrived with Ryklof van Goens the elder, who had been appointed Governor-General of Netherlands India in 1678 and who had been a Commissioner in van Riebeeck's time. He was on his way back to Holland to recover his health. Although in poor health, he managed a visit to Stellenbosch where he made a number of directions with regard to crops. Experiments were to be made in the growing of flax, hemp and indigo with a view to extending trade but none had turned out to be successful. He had reinforced the prohibition on the growing of tobacco because the VOC's existing trade was very profitable, and reiterated the prudence of the growth of more wheat to lessen the need for imported rice from the East.

Later in the year, ever mindful of the desirability of improving trade in the broadest sense, the Council of Policy decided to set up a new market place on Saturdays in the present Greenmarket Square in Cape Town, and no other market was allowed to compete. The range of produce for sale was extensive and included game and wildfowl supplied by those licensed to shoot. There were supplies of meat and poultry, dairy products, vegetables, fruit, fresh and dried fish, penguin and duiker (long-tailed cormorants) eggs. Subsequently, van Goens was able to inspect the castle where he agreed with van der Stel that the main gate of the castle should be walled up since it faced onto the sea and the surf tended to be heavy. Instead, the gate was moved to the west side facing the parade, where it has been ever since.

From time to time, there had been discussion between the Governor General and the Commander about the possibility of using False Bay as a winter anchorage in preference to the storm-ridden Table Bay, where the strong north west winds were a hazard from May to August. However, they decided it would be too difficult for handling cargo and too isolated for the ships' crews. There was also no obvious water supply. The Commander had named the inlet Simon's Bay but it was not until the middle of the eighteenth century that False Bay became a winter anchorage. Governor General van Goens stayed for over two months at the Cape, dying soon after his return to the Netherlands.

An innovative development, instigated by Simon van der Stel, took place when, in 1683, some new grazing was organised at Klapmuts, between Cape Town and what was later to become the wine town of Paarl. This alternative pasture enabled the cattle at Hottentots Holland to have a change of grazing. The following year, the VOC was able to stop sending cattle trading expeditions further inland by handing over that responsibility to the Khoi chief known as Captain Klaas, who purchased large herds at very good rates and in return kept one head of cattle out of every five for himself. The number of cattle and sheep which became available made it necessary for the Company to open up further grazing areas. Outposts were therefore established at Visser's Hoek, Riet Vlie, Diep River and Kuilen, with a few soldiers and slaves left to guard these new grazings.

In the same year, van der Stel turned his concern to the depletion of native timber from the wooded valleys on the overland route to Hout Bay. The increasing demand for timber for construction made it all the more necessary to manage the chief forests efficiently. The difficulty of moving timber around from the Cape forests had earlier led to the observation that it would be cheaper and simpler to have the timber shipped in from Holland. He appointed three burgher sawyers to take charge of the forest at Hout Bay, situated on its inlet on the west side of the Cape peninsula facing the turbulent waters of the Atlantic.

The sawyers were given a ten-year contract to supply the Company's needs and they had instructions to seek out those burghers who had a licence to purchase. By this time, the cart track leading from Cape Town to Hout Bay had been improved and it could be used, with difficulty, by oxen-hauled wagons laden with timber. The indigenous yellow wood in particular was much in demand for construction purposes because it made excellent planks suitable for floors and roof beams in the building of houses and it could be managed by the sawyers.

Simon van der Stel's interest in botany made him an enthusiast for replanting trees. He used a wide variety of tree seedlings, both from Europe and the East, in the nurseries of the Company's garden: "of them all none seemed to thrive like the oak." Later he issued instructions that every farmer was to plant at least one hundred oaks and he himself set the example at Constantia and on the Company's farms. In the spring of 1687, he had the satisfaction of seeing between four thousand and five thousand oaks already starting to bear acorns in the Cape and Stellenbosch districts. The Commander had over fifty thousand trees in the nurseries awaiting planting out from the enlarged Company's garden at Rondebosch. It was made a stipulation that everyone taking up land at Stellenbosch was required to plant trees.

Another Ryklof van Goens visitation took place in October 1684 when the younger van Goens, Ordinary Councillor of India, and son of the Governor General, anchored in Saldanha Bay, on the way from Holland to the East. On the grounds that he was too unwell to complete the journey into Table Bay, he had asked that the Commander would fetch him overland. The sixty-mile journey through the sandy scrub to Cape Town must have been a nightmare in the circumstances but the details were not recorded. The Commander put up van Goens and his wife at Rustenburg, the Company's country house, where he remained in poor health

PLATE 1

A States Yacht in a fresh breeze running towards a group of Dutch ships
(Painting by Willem van de Velde the Younger, 1673 © National Maritime Museum, London)

In the painting, a large group of Dutch ships are gathered under a stormy sky. This may record the assembling of some of the Dutch fleet off the Texel in 1672. Admiral de Ruyter put to sea in late April or early May and Cornelis de Witt, the Ruwaard of Putten, joined de Ruyter's ship as the States-General representative. In the right foreground is a sprit rigged States yacht, probably the yacht of the States-General shown sailing towards de Ruyter's flagship the 'Zeven Provincien'.

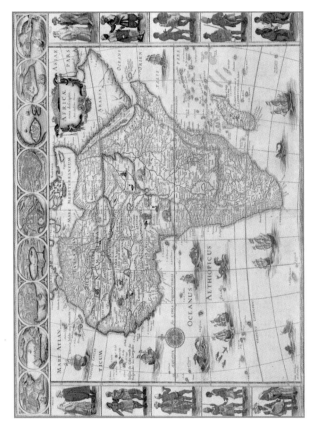

PLATE 2

Africae, Guillaume Blaeu, Amsterdam 1619 to c.1650

Courtesy of Jonathan Potter Limited

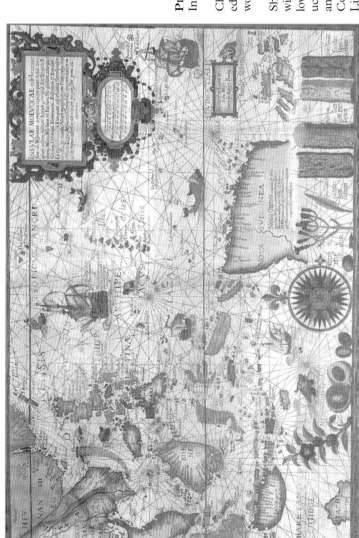

PLATE 3
Insulae Moluccae

Chart from the English
edition of Linschoten's
work, London 1598

Shows the Spice Islands
with illustrations along the
lower margin of local products: nutmeg, mace, cloves
and sandalwood
Courtesy of Jonathan Potter
Limited

PLATE 4
Jan van Riebeeck
Courtesy of the Iziko William Fehr Collection, Cape Town Castle

PLATE 5
Maria de la Quellerie, wife of Jan van Riebeeck
Courtesy of the Iziko William Fehr Collection, Cape Town Castle

PLATE 6
Arrival at the
Cape of Jan van
Riebeeck
Painted by
Charles Bell in
1850
Courtesy of the
National Library
of South Africa

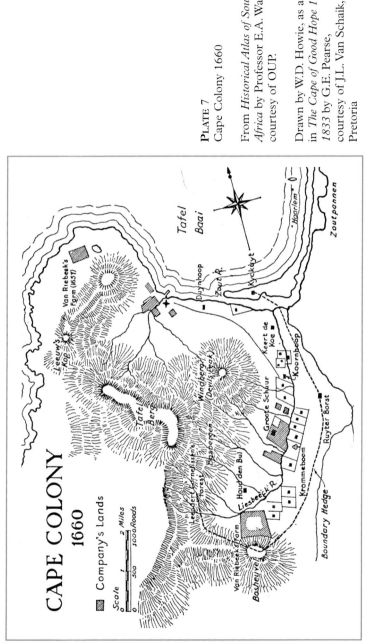

PLATE 7
Cape Colony 1660

From *Historical Atlas of South Africa* by Professor E.A. Walker, courtesy of OUP.

Drawn by W.D. Howie, as adapted in *The Cape of Good Hope 1652-1833* by G.E. Pearse, courtesy of J.L. Van Schaik, Pretoria

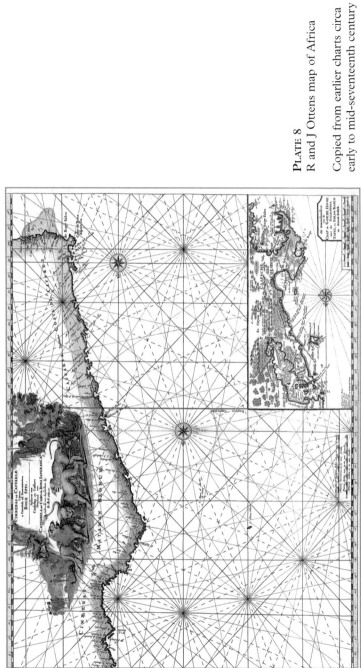

PLATE 8
R and J Ottens map of Africa

Copied from earlier charts circa
early to mid–seventeenth century

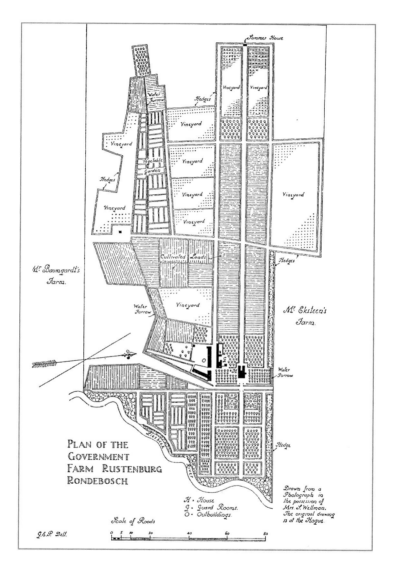

FIGURE 9 Plan of the Government Farm, Rustenburg,
Rondebosch. Shows the house, guard rooms and summer house at
the end of central walk. From *The Cape of Good Hope 1652-1833* by
G.E. Pearse, 1956 (courtesy of J.L. Van Schaik, Pretoria).

for the length of his visit, which had to be extended on medical grounds. On 18 December he travelled with his wife to the castle, intending to go on to Ceylon, and on 26 December he embarked from a sedan chair. Three days later he reappeared, unable to cope with the rough sea. He returned to Rustenburg "to await the restoration of health." However, he was able to attend a Council session in early March 1685 before finally leaving for the East in May.

While at the Cape, he had assumed authority over the Commander and he took it upon himself to make a number of grants of land to those who had requested it. Van Goens seemed to have been impressed by the Commander's son, Adriaan van der Stel, who had become a burgher and been granted land in full ownership. Van Goens granted him privileges including the rights to catch fish in False Bay without having to pay any tax, and to shoot birds and game as he liked. At the instigation of van Goens, these and other considerable privileges were ratified by the Council but these freedoms were not well received by the other burghers, who thought the young van der Stel had been unreasonably favoured. By contrast, they were restricted to shoot no more than could be eaten by the farmer and his family, and in one year the total permitted kill was one rhinoceros, a hippopotamus, an eland and a hartebeest.

In the following year, on 19 April 1685, a High Commissioner, specially appointed by the Lords Seventeen, arrived at the Cape. He was Hendrik Adriaan van Rheede tot Drakenstein, usually known as Lord Mydrecht. Nobly born and generally a much more civilised man than many of those working for the VOC, he was liked and respected by Simon van der Stel. They worked closely together during the three months he spent at the Cape. Van Rheede had been appointed Councillor of India and was on his way to Ceylon to investigate charges of corruption. Before leaving Holland, the Seventeen had as usual instructed him to investigate and put right anything he found wrong at the Cape, where he was acting as their personal emissary. One of his first acts had been to invite any local inhabitant who had a grievance to express it.

He looked into the running of the different public bodies and found they were fulfilling their functions well. In consequence, no changes were called for in the Burgher Council, the Church Council, the Board of Militia, the Matrimonial Court, the Orphan Court, and the Court of Commissioners for Petty Cases. The Council of Policy, which had proved to be an effective body from its early foundation by van Riebeeck, was enlarged to eight members. They consisted of the Commander, who acted as President, the sekunde, the two senior military officers, the fiscal and the treasurer, the chief salesman and the garrison book keeper. In this varied group, all aspects of the administration of affairs at the Cape were covered. In Stellenbosch, a number of administrative changes had been made as a result of the growth of the community. The local court, administered by the 'landdrost', who was in charge of the Company's interests and who supervised the VOC farms and cattle grazing outposts in the area, was to be assisted by two other Dutchmen and was to be provided with a horse and slave. Part of the landdrost's responsibilities was to maintain public order, cause roads to be repaired and to supervise proceedings in the manner of a district council. It was necessary to build a corn mill and its cost was to be met by levying a tax on the sheep and cattle. On his last day at the Cape, the Lord Mydrecht appointed the first landdrost of Stellenbosch, Johannes Mulder, a Dutchman of good reputation, and he was to be joined by four burghers, Gerrit van der Byl, Henning Huising, Jan Mostert, and Herman Smit, as 'heemraaden', or administrators.

During his visit, the High Commissioner had investigated the keeping of slaves and made a number of new laws concerning their emancipation: Every male half-breed could claim freedom as a right at the age of twenty five years and every female half-breed at the age of twenty two years, provided only that he or she professed Christianity and spoke the Dutch language. The education of slave children under the age of twelve years was to be provided for. Such provisions were fairly predictable and the pupils were required to attend school where they would be taught the basic principles of Christianity according to the approach of the Dutch Reformed Church, the ability to read and write, and to conduct themselves respectfully towards their superiors. Racist policies over marriage were enacted and 'marriage between Europeans and freed slaves of full colour' was prohibited but Europeans and half-breeds could marry if they chose. At this time, relations between the Dutch settlers and the Khoi were more amicable than had often been the case earlier when the Khoi had found the Dutch usurping their traditional seasonal grazing grounds.

The comparative lack of enterprise in the slow growth of the Cape settlement in its early years was in marked contrast to the rapid growth of settlers in North America. Between 1630 and 1642, about six thousand settlers arrived in Massachusetts Bay. Among the reasons for this influx to North America from England were religious persecution at home and the lure of a new land free from home interference. The basis for the growth of the Dutch colonies in North America was totally different and was related to the expansion of trade between the old and the new worlds. The fur trade was a case in point. In 1612, Dutch merchants were trading on Manhattan Island and, in that year, the Dutch West India Company had been founded with powers similar to the VOC, although the Company never measured up to the size and complexity of its vastly greater sister organisation.

In 1626, the Director General of the Dutch West India Company, Pieter Minuit, had bought Manhattan Island for the sum of twenty four dollars from the Indians and had established New Amsterdam. The Company also settled in Connecticut, Delaware, Pennsylvania and New Jersey. Moreover, operating over large areas of coastal North and South America, the Dutch had succeeded in wresting the sugar and slave trade from the Portuguese. Also of importance was the desirability of intercepting Spanish ships and purloining their cargoes bound for Europe, especially gold.

By contrast, the Cape did not represent a new way of life and the migrants who went there were sent by the VOC and were subject to its many rules and regulations. In addition, there was a lack of incentive to migrate from Holland, where skilled employment was secure due to the rich and diverse market place. It was characteristic of the cost conscious VOC that nothing was done to encourage the decorative arts in the Cape at their expense. In keeping with the policy of the Seventeen to run the Cape as cheaply as possible, none of the great Dutch landscape painters went to work at the Cape. This might be considered surprising in view of the stunning beauty of Table Bay with Table Mountain as a backdrop to a maritime scene. The only known seventeenth century example is a painting of ships in Table Bay by Aernout Smit in 1683 during Simon van der Stel's time. The picture hangs in the Iziko William Fehr collection in the castle at Cape Town. There are two paintings depicting VOC possessions in the East which give an immediate indication of the splendour associated with their more favoured centres of trade in comparison with the Cape. These pictures, which now hang in the Rijksmuseum in Amsterdam, portray the Batavia Kasteel, with its elegant palm trees, painted by A. Beeckman in 1656, and a splendid VOC settlement on the Hooghly in Bengal, painted in 1665 by H. van Schuylenburgh. These views would have been known to the High Commissioner Lord Mydrecht from his travels in the East.

During the visit of High Commissioner Lord Mydrecht to the Cape, a French ship had sailed into Table Bay in June 1685. An unusual event in itself, speculation had increased when it was learned that among the passengers was the French Ambassador to the Court of Siam and his entourage. There were also six Jesuit missionaries, one of whom, Father Guy Tachard, was an

FIGURE 10 The VOC Factory at Hooghly, Bengal. Painted by Hendrik van Schuylenburgh (Reproduced courtesy of the Rijksmuseum, Amsterdam).

astronomer. They were welcomed in a friendly manner by the High Commissioner and the Commander, van der Stel, although it had been made clear that mass could not be said on their ship nor on shore. The Commander gave them accommodation in a garden pavilion at the entrance to the Company's garden. The pavilion's platform roof could be used as an observatory for Father Tachard's twelve foot long telescope. With their instruments, which were the best of the day, the Frenchmen made calculations to measure longitude and their readings were fairly accurate.

It soon became apparent that the Jesuits were engaged in a form of espionage. Any information they could obtain about the VOC operations at the Cape was important to them. They had particularly sought the help of Heinrich Claudius, who was not only a VOC physician but a talented draughtsman and artist, highly skilled at drawing plants; he was also a map maker. He had given a map and much information to Father Tachard so that when the priest's book was published in Paris in 1686, all Claudius's information was revealed. Appreciative of the assistance of the High Commissioner and the Commander, the book described the Commander's house as "a double storeyed house, stone built with balconies and iron balustrades, and a large hall, used as a church on Sundays." Claudius was eventually deported in disgrace.

High Commissioner Lord Mydrecht and the Commander van der Stel clearly had a good working relationship and the Commander had appreciated the cultivated approach of this visitor and the understanding which he had shown. Van der Stel was anxious to establish for himself an area of land where he could farm and set up trade. A keen agriculturist from years of experience, he had looked at a number of sites on the good land southeast of the castle in Cape Town from where earlier settlers had, in the main, moved to Stellenbosch. In conjunction with the High Commissioner, the boundaries had been chosen, measured and a plan had been drawn up. On 13 July 1685, the title to the land was

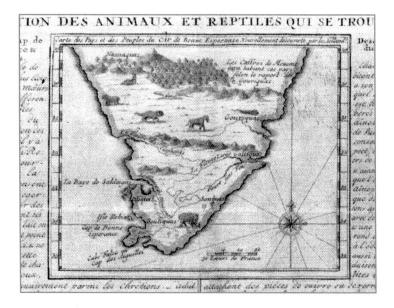

FIGURE 11 Map of South Africa. Drawn by Hendrik Claudius
who accompanied Simon van der Stel to Namaqualand in 1685.
From Tachard's account of his visit to the East, published in *Atlas
Historique* by H.A. Chatelaine in 1719.

issued and 891 morgen (about 2000 acres) of land were agreed
in the title. The Commander named the farm Constantia but the
reason for the choice of name was never clear. Different attribu-
tions have been made including Lord Mydrecht's invalid grand-
daughter and another name of Simon van der Stel's wife Jacoba,
who died in Amsterdam in 1700.

The site of Groot Constantia had been chosen by van der Stel
after buckets of soil had been dug up in a line from Table Bay to
False Bay, from which samples had been analysed at the castle.
The land lying between Wynberg and Steenberg had proved to be
the most fertile. Van der Stel had walked over the area and chosen

FIGURE 12 The Jesuits' Observatory at the Cape. Shows 12 foot telescope used by Father Tachard. Drawn by C. Vermeulen

a site for the house, which had a spectacular view over gently falling ground towards False Bay. The site was sheltered from the wind by the southerly extension of Table Mountain, known as the Twelve Apostles.

In the same year, 1685, the Commander laid out the largest vineyard in the Cape at Constantia and he experimented with seeds and cuttings grown from the Company's garden. The farm did well and produced the best wine in the Cape. Although competition in this respect was not strong, the quality of Constantia wine was to become famous and was the only wine referred to by name by Jane Austen in the novel 'Sense and Sensibility'. By the time of the vintage year of 1698, Constantia was regularly producing quality wines meriting export to Europe, which were carefully watched over in person by van der Stel himself. François Valentyn, the French traveller, clergyman and author, who visited the Cape in 1685, 1695, 1705 and 1714, and wrote a great work on Dutch possessions in India, praised the development of Groot Constantia as "an exceptionally well planned estate on which grows all the choicest wine to be found at the Cape."

Always the task of a visiting Commissioner to inspect on behalf of the VOC developments taking place at the Cape, the investigations of van Rheede had been particularly thorough. The treatment of slaves had especially exercised him and he ruled that clearly defined land reserves should be made available to them. Moreover, slaves brought into the country from abroad should be freed after thirty years of service and slaves born in slavery at the Cape should be freed after forty years. Van Rheede had noted that male slaves more than ever outnumbered their masters. He was also concerned with the state of the free burghers. He had made a rough count of the burgher population and found, in an area close to the castle, about thirty families entirely made up, rather surprisingly, of gardeners, artisans and innkeepers. Further off, there were twenty four families established between Rondebosch and Wynberg engaged in farming. The greatest number of free burghers, about one hundred families, had moved from the Cape peninsula to the more recently developed areas near Stellenbosch. Van Rheede had been pleased to learn that over fourteen thousand sheep and two thousand cattle in this area were owned by the free burghers whom he saw as constructive colonists.

The Lord Mydrecht had also been pleased with the Company's garden, which Simon van der Stel had inherited in Table Valley. The garden was essentially a place where fruits and vegetables were produced according to the purpose for which the garden had been laid out by van Riebeeck, nearly thirty years earlier. By the time Simon van der Stel had taken over, the gardens were becoming decorative as well as productive. A knowledgeable botanist, he had decided to widen the scope of the garden and to include a number of more exotic plants and shrubs. He was aware of the significance of the Hortus Botanicus in Leiden, founded in 1587, which was the earliest in Europe. A number of plant collections were sent to Leiden from the Cape, especially after the construction of greenhouses in 1686, which created a micro-climate in which sun-loving plants from the Cape could flourish. The Commander divided up the garden into a number of rectangular sections, protected from the wind by hedges. Some years after van der Stel had laid out the garden afresh, "visitors who had seen the most celebrated gardens of Europe and India, were agreed that nowhere else in the world was so great a variety of trees and shrubs, of vegetables and flowers, to be met together." Among the visitors to the garden in 1685, on his second visit to the Cape, was the ever inquisitive French priest, Father Tachard. His comments reflected a comparison with France where garden designs of Le Nôtre at Versailles and Vaux-le-Vicomte would have been familiar to him. The French priest wrote:

"The garden measures one thousand four hundred and eleven ordinary paces in length, and two hundred and thirty-five in breadth. Its beauty is not made up of flower beds or playing waters, as in France. But one could have them as well, if the Dutch Company would spare the expense, for there is a rivulet of live water flowing down the mountain and crossing the garden. However, one sees here avenues, as far as the eye can reach, of lemon, pomegranate and orange trees, all of them planted in open ground, and sheltered from the wind by high and thick palisades of a kind of bay tree which they call spek, being evergreen and rather resembling the filaria. By the arrangement of the avenues this garden is divided into mediocre squares. Some of them are full of fruit trees, among which one observes, besides apple, pear, quince and apricot trees and other excellent fruits from Europe, also pine-apples, bananas and several other kinds bearing the rarest fruits, and which are found in all parts of the world and have been transported to the garden and are grown there with great care. The other squares have been sown with various 'roots' (carrots, turnips, etc.), legumes and herbs, some others with the most favourite flowers of Europe and other kinds which we do not know and which are of a peculiar fragrance and beauty. The Gentlemen of the East India Company, to whom the garden belongs, as we have said before, had laid it out in order to have it always on this spot like a Storehouse of all sorts of refreshments for their ships sailing for the Indies or returning from there, and which never fail to touch at the Cape of Good Hope."

It was recorded that over one hundred slaves were employed in the gardens under the supervision of a head gardener. Appointed supervisor of the Company's garden by Simon van der Stel around 1680, Hendrik Bernard Oldenland was ideal for the task. He was an eminent botanist, who had studied medicine for three years at Leiden University under Professor Paul Hermann when the study of medicine and botany were closely allied. He made several botanic expeditions inland from the Cape where he had collected wild flowers and plants for study in the Company's garden and in the herbarium at Leiden. Correspondence with the

Seventeen always stressed the importance of using ships belonging to the Chamber of Delft for the transport of plants to Leiden as being the most reliable passage. Experience had shown that ships from other chambers, less convenient for Leiden, were not so dependable and plant cargoes had been lost. An exuberant impression of the garden was written a few years later by the Rev. John Ovington, a clergyman from England, who visited the Cape in 1689, after Simon van der Stel's improvements had matured. He wrote:

> "The tam'd garden abundantly supplies the ships with variety of roots and green herbs, which contribute not a little to the health and even preservation of life on these tedious Eastern voyages. Here is the variety of excellent fruits, of pulses and roots, which either Europe or Asia afford. Here are those large walks, those stately hedges and alleys of cypress, and beds of flowers, which make it beautiful and pleasant as the garden of a prince, and useful as that of a peasant. The garden in all its walks is kept so very neat and clean, that even in the winter seasons scarce a leaf is seen upon the ground. The trees are curiously prun'd and the hedges trimm'd with such exactness that no one irregular excescence appears, or branch shooting out beyond his fellow. Much of the fruit in it comes to maturity twice a year, and many trees by their nearness to the sun are verdant and beautiful all the year."

However, a discordant note had been struck when certain criticisms of the Commander had been made to van Rheede, who had consequently had a frank discussion with van der Stel about these complaints. Although the Commander was much respected by the community and usually considered fair in his dealings, van Rheede had stressed to him the importance of kindness and a caring attitude at all times in the Commander's leadership and the need to be strict with those whose behaviour was dishonest and disruptive.

Among the many topics discussed between the Commander and the High Commissioner was the legend that there were copper deposits in Namaqualand, an area away to the north. Earlier expeditions had produced no certainty and van der Stel had found this tantalizing. Van Rheede gave permission for the Commander to be absent from the normal duties of his post in order to lead a fresh expedition.

CHAPTER 10

In Search of Copper

By 25 August 1685, a month after the departure to India of the Lord Mydrecht, detailed arrangements for van der Stel's expedition were in place and the party started off northwards into the interior towards Namaqualand. The main train of wagons left in the morning and the Commander himself left on horseback in the afternoon. The whole operation was on a much grander scale than anything that had been attempted before. The wheeled traffic comprised fifteen wagons, each drawn by eight oxen, eight carts and one coach. Of the wagons, eight would go only as far as the Elephant River because they belonged to the burghers. In addition to the draught animals, there were two hundred spare oxen, many of them trained as pack animals, thirteen horses, and eight mules. The equipment also included a boat for crossing the Elephant and Berg rivers and two small cannons to impress the natives with their pop-gun effect.

The number of personnel in the expedition was large and varied, consisting of the Commander and three slaves as attendants, fifty-six Europeans, including soldiers, forty six drivers and leaders, who were mostly of mixed race, and a Macassar prisoner of state with an accompanying slave, together with some Khoi to act as interpreters. The expedition aimed at the Berg river valley, which it reached on 31 August and a camp was set up at Misverstand Ford. The next morning, after prayers, the boat was launched on the river to ferry the baggage across, an exercise which took two days. While this was going on, a party went ahead in search of meat and fortunately returned to the camp well stocked with oxen and sheep. On the second day, a group of five Khoi were seen but they ran off on catching sight of the Europeans. However, they came back on being presented with pipes and tobacco by a sergeant. It was made clear that they lived on honey and game and that they were following an eland, which they had wounded the previous day with a poisoned arrow. The Commander had offered them a sheep, which they had immediately killed and dismembered before cooking it on the hot ashes of a fire. This could be seen as an early example of a 'braai.'

The party was proceeding on its way on the following day when it startled a huge rhinoceros, which made a direct charge at the Commander's carriage. The Commander had jumped out of the way and the beast was headed off by inaccurate musket fire which did it no harm. Some days later, on 9 September, the Little Elephant River was reached, lying in a dry and less fertile area where several elephants were seen. The next major stop was made in a more hospitable place where water, grass, trees and game were to be seen. Nearby, there was a hill which they named Uilenberg on account of the number of owls seen there. On the following day, they moved on to the Elephant River and made ready to cross it in the boat. The burghers turned back, having collected a satisfactory stock of meat for future use. The river crossing occupied three days and the party was able to move on again on 18 September. It had cheered the party to note that the seasonable weather was a marked contrast to the drought conditions of the previous four years. Where earlier explorers had found parched conditions, there were now streams and grass. Hares and antelopes could be seen in the long grass and the special hunting skill of the Khoi was demonstrated in bringing down flying quails with sticks. The Commander planned that an advance party would always go ahead of the main party so as to choose the best route for the wagons, where indeed any choice existed, and to select the next camp site. On arrival, the oxen were turned loose to graze and rest. Each morning and evening, the company assembled for prayers and the reading of scripture. On 20 September, the expedition found themselves in a narrow

FIGURE 13 Later stylised drawing of Khoisan activities.
(Reproduced by permission of the National Library of South Africa).

defile, with the Elephant River on one side of them and a steep rock face on the other. A group of Khoi were in the midst of a dispute with their chief. The Commander, to his credit, was able to restore peace among them after several days of diplomacy, and bought a number of cattle from them.

During the following week, the countryside became more barren each day and the conditions for survival more difficult. Although the water was salty, there was enough grass for the cattle to graze. There was a lack of firewood because there were no trees. On 29 September, however, the party reached the Little Dorn Bosch River and it was noted that the sea could be seen "about twenty eight English miles away." The following day saw the arrival of the explorers at the Great Dorn Bosch River, which proved to be a deep and fast flowing stream. While they were there, a group of Khoi visited the camp and were given a sheep and some brandy. It was noted that "they were wretchedly thin, for they were living on nothing better than tortoises, caterpillars, locusts, and bulbs of plants. They made very merry over the feast provided for them, and danced and sang right joyfully. The treatment they received was so much to their liking that for some days they accompanied the expedition, making themselves useful as guides."

Contact with a group of the Namaquas was made on 4 October when their kraals were spotted. The Commander entertained the chiefs and their wives with European food but it was evident that they preferred brandy and tobacco. While discussing possible trading plans, the Commander gave an undertaking to prevent the Cape Khoi from attacking the Namaquas. By this time, the landscape had again become so rugged that progress was slow and difficult. The expedition was given an entertainment by a group of Namaquas with music and dancing, with reeds of different lengths providing the music. "A master musician stood in the centre, having a long rod in his hand with which he gave directions, singing a tune and beating with his foot as well." The players kept leaping up and down but produced music which surprised the Europeans by its harmony and power. Outside was a deep circle of men and women dancing and clapping their hands in time with the music. This entertainment continued until evening, when the Commander had an ox slaughtered for his visitors, and distributed a small keg of arrack among them.

The expedition began to move again on 16 October and for the following five days the route was very heavy going and through such difficult terrain that their wagons and carts were often overturned. However, the Commander's resolution paid off and, on 21 October, the party arrived at the Copper Mountain and pitched camp. Van der Stel noted that the distance from the castle was over three hundred miles. A fortnight was spent in extracting copper ore and investigating the locality, which was arid and desolate. However, copper ore was discovered in abundance and of surprising richness.

On 5 November, the Commander decided to explore the area between the Copper Mountain and the sea and camp was broken for the purpose. It was evident that the route was rough and arid, with a lack of water. Morale among the explorers was not high and a number of them were in favour of going home. However, van der Stel insisted that he wished to study the coastline, hoping to discover a harbour. On 17 November, the advance party reached the coast and five days later the complete party camped near the mouth of an almost dry river bed. An attempt to explore the coastline further north from 22 November to 2 December was handicapped persistently by heavy surf along the shore and there was a complete lack of any potential harbour. There was no supply of fresh water and this posed an acute problem to the explorers. The cattle were hard hit: "some of them ran into the sea and drank and immediately afterwards died." On 12 December, the Commander called a halt to further exploring and the party turned for home, much to everyone's relief. But the return journey was not easy and under the midsummer sun it took eighteen days to get back to the Elephant River, the party sometimes moving at night when it was cooler. Four days were spent watering the stock at the Elephant River during which time some local exploration of the coast revealed an inlet, which was later named Lambert's Bay.

After an absence of five months and one day, the party arrived back at the castle on 26 January 1686. Copper had indeed been found in Namaqualand. The legend was proved by Simon van der Stel's well organised expedition but it was too remote for commercial exploitation in those conditions. Not until 1852 was mining undertaken, development becoming easier after the coming of the railways in the 1870s. Copper was the first mineral to attract the attention of the Europeans in the Cape. It was no mean achievement on the part of Simon van der Stel to have proved its existence by 1685.

CHAPTER 11

Arrival of the Huguenots

Not long after his return from the Namaqualand copper expedition, Simon van der Stel had to cope with another French visitation. Admiral de Vaudricourt dropped anchor in Table Bay on his way home to France from Siam in March 1686. On board were the Ambassador de Chaumont, the Abbot de Choisy, and Father Tachard. This time, they were greeted a little nervously "with cautious civility." Still bent on gathering strategic information for the King of France, Louis XIV, Father Tachard climbed Table Mountain with another priest and a guide. He mapped the outlook over Table Bay from the top and made notes. In order to restrict his activities, the Commander put him up at the Company's country house at Rustenburg, which was further away than the observatory where he had stayed on previous visits and which he was told was under repair.

The following year, the French Admiral called yet again on his return from France. This time he had a fleet of six ships containing over three hundred sick people and a detachment of six hundred men as had been requested by the King of Siam. Through a Council of Policy meeting, the Commander declared, as a defence precaution, that not more than sixty of the sick French passengers might come on shore at the same time. And those who were healthy were not to be on shore between sunset and sunrise. As a further precaution to strengthen the garrison, the country militia was alerted and forty farmers reported for duty at the castle after completing the sowing of their grain crops at Stellenbosch. They had been instructed that: "no one shall dare to leave the castle at night." In the event, their military services were not needed and the French fleet sailed for Siam without causing any problems, at the end of June.

Meanwhile in France, Louis XIV had caused turmoil amongst his Protestant subjects by the revocation in 1685 of the Edict of Nantes. Under Henri IV, originally a Huguenot himself, the Edict of Nantes in 1598 had granted some toleration and certain rights to the Huguenots. Following the revocation, a flood of Huguenots immediately began to flee the country taking with them whatever possessions they could carry. The knowledge that Protestants were secure in Holland made this a haven sought by a large number of them. Commercial enterprise there was already strong but there was not room for accommodating a great number of arrivals from France on a permanent basis. The VOC saw the possibility of sending some of the French to the Cape where their well-known practical skills could be of benefit to the community there.

The offer of free passage and grants of land were a practical inducement to Huguenot settlers and, in 1688, the first of them arrived. Like refugees the world over, some of them had reached the Netherlands utterly destitute. The Council of Seventeen hoped the Huguenots would supply such skills as were lacking in the Dutch. They underlined the importance of knowledge in wheat growing and cattle rearing as well as the making of wine, brandy, and the growing of olives. Some of the Huguenots were certainly experts in these areas and would fill an economic need at the Cape. For the six thousand mile journey from Holland to the Cape, shipping arrangements were made by the different Chambers of the VOC so that families and friends could travel together as far as possible. Five ships carried the Huguenots to South Africa, the vessels *Voorschoten, Borssenburg, Oosterland, China* and *Zuid Beveland.*

The *Voorschoten* sailed from Delfthaven on 31 December 1687 with twenty three emigrants, including Charles Marais of Plessis, accompanied by his wife Catherine and their four sons whose ages ranged from twenty four down to six. Another family was that of Phillipe Fouche, his wife Anne and their three children of whom the oldest was aged six. Of the eleven other passengers, only two were women, one unmarried. The preponderance of men among the migrants was a source of constant concern to Simon van der Stel, who was anxious to secure a more balanced pattern of settlement. The *Borssenburg* sailed on 6 January 1688, but no trace of her passenger list remains either in the Cape or the Hague archives. Later in the same month, the *Oosterland* sailed on 29 January from Middelburg with twenty four Huguenot emigrants of whom the Taillefer family accounted for eight, with Isaac Taillefer, a vine dresser, his wife Susanne and their six children aged between fourteen and one. The de Savoye family also consisted of six. Otherwise there were two married couples, Jean Prieur du Plessis, a surgeon from Poitiers, and his wife Madeleine and David Nortier, a carpenter, and his wife Marie. One unmarried young woman and five bachelors completed the company.

After some delay, the *China* sailed from Rotterdam on 20 March 1688 with forty two passengers. The ship was crowded and the weather stormy, with the voyage taking longer as a result. The passengers included Jean Mesnard, his wife Louise and their six children, ranging in age from ten years to five months.

Two little girls, Marie Roux, aged ten, and her sister Marguerite, aged seven, were travelling with their bachelor uncles Jean and Pierre Jourdan. Pierre Joubert and his wife Isabeau, and a young unmarried woman, Susanne René, were among the passengers together with eight young women from the Orphan Chamber at Rotterdam, who had agreed to emigrate to South Africa. They were said to be "of unblemished reputation, industrious and skilled at farm work." All of them married within a few months of their arrival. Such marriages pleased Simon van der Stel, who was glad to see an increase in family life at the Cape, especially among the Dutch settlers. The voyage of the *China* had been long and difficult and when she arrived in Table Bay on 4 August, both crew and passengers were mostly ill. Twenty passengers had died on the voyage, including twelve of the French refugees. The last group of Huguenots sailed on the *Zuid Beveland* from Middelburg on 22 April 1688 and had an easier and quicker passage than those who had travelled on the *China*. As in the case of the *Borssenburg*, the passenger list has been lost. The *Zuid Beveland* brought the pastor Pierre Simond and his wife Anne from Zierickzee to be the first Protestant minister to the French refugees.

At the time of the arrival of the Huguenot refugees, who had neither property nor funds, the settlement inland was very sparse. Stellenbosch was still a small village and the population of the area chiefly lived in isolated homesteads scattered over the countryside. The Cape inhabitants gave a warm welcome to the Huguenots for whom they had raised a collection of money to help them over their financial difficulties while they settled in to the new environment. The VOC had sent out some basic provisions for the new settlers, which included salt meat, peas and ship's biscuit to keep them going during the first weeks after their arrival at the Cape. This food supply must have seemed depressingly austere to those accustomed to the standard and variety of French provincial cooking. Bearing in mind that the French and Dutch were not always at peace with one another, the Huguenots had been obliged to swear allegiance to the Dutch before leaving for South Africa. Simon van der Stel was prepared to welcome the newcomers but he was innately suspicious that the French could be a disrupting influence among the earlier Dutch settlers. To help with the transporting of the new arrivals from Table Bay to Stellenbosch, the Burgher Council provided six wagons and timber was supplied from Holland for the construction of temporary housing.

The Huguenots were given land in some of the most beautiful areas of the Cape, partly near Stellenbosch, and along the wide floor of the Berg River, a region which the Commander had named Drakenstein after the recent visit of the High Commissioner, van Rheede, Lord Mydrecht. The new settlers were experienced wine farmers and were the first to improve the questionable reputation of Cape wine. Objecting to van der Stel's policy of distributing them among the Dutch farmers, some Huguenots moved nearer their friends in a part of the Drakenstein valley, which came to be known as Franschhoek (French Corner). This sheltered pocket lies in the upper Berg valley at the foot of Du Toit's Kloof pass. It was understandable that the French settlers preferred not to be split up and to be able to develop their considerable agricultural skills among themselves. More than a dozen grants of land for viticulture were made to the Huguenot settlers in the Franschhoek area in the early years of their settlement from 1688, one of the first being Boschendal. Among grants of land made by van der Stel were those at Steenberg in 1688, Bellingham in 1693, and La Bri and Haute Provence in 1694. All played a significant part in the development of the Cape wine production of today.

After their departure from Europe, the Huguenots continued to set great store by their protestant worship and their contact with Pastor Simond. It was arranged that he should preach in French on alternate Sundays at Stellenbosch and at a burgher's house at Drakenstein. Linked to this plan was the reading of a sermon and prayers in Dutch by the 'sick comforter,' or pastoral visitor, when Pastor Simond was at the other venue.

The refugees began to establish themselves and to build simple houses straightaway. For many of them, such tasks were well within their ability; for others, such as the surgeon from Poitiers, Jean Prieur du Plessis, and the merchant Jacques de Savoye, life was more difficult at first. The VOC wanted to provide slaves to help in the construction work but none were immediately available. One of the first matters to be pursued was the education of Huguenot children. The Commander was sympathetic to this request and, in November 1688, the first schoolmaster was appointed at Drakenstein. He was Paul Roux from Orange, who understood both the French and Dutch languages. In addition to his school duties, he was also appointed church clerk.

A second arrival of Huguenots took place in 1689, with the anchoring in Table Bay of the *Wapen van Alkmaar* at the end of January and the *Zion* early in May. The arrival of these ships brought the total of Huguenot settlers to over one hundred and thirty. Among the arrivals on the *Zion* were the three de Villiers brothers, Abraham, Pierre and Jacob. Abraham's particular skills in viticulture had become known to the Council of Seventeen, which sent a letter of recommendation to Simon van der Stel. It was Abraham who later became the main builder of the homestead Boschendal, a property which remained in the de Villiers family until 1875.

Later in the same year, 1689, Jacques de Savoye, who had been appointed a 'heemraad' at Stellenbosch, found himself part of a deputation to the Commander on religious grounds. In November, he and four others, Pastor Simond, Lotus Cordier, Daniel de Ruelle and Abraham de Villiers presented themselves to Simon van der Stel at the castle. They made representation that the Huguenots should be allowed to set up their own church at Drakenstein and cease to be part of the church at Stellenbosch. The Commander had become extremely angry at what he saw as a separatist movement on the part of the French, whom he never wholly trusted in any case. He ruled that there should be no such development and reminded them that they had taken the oath of allegiance and that they would remain a branch of the church at Stellenbosch. Pastor Simond had written some months previously to the Council of Seventeen about this grievance of the French and was awaiting a reply. When it came, in June 1691, the reply was highly diplomatic, being acceptable both to the Commander and the Huguenots. It authorised the Huguenots to have their own congregations in both Stellenbosch and Drakenstein, which pleased them, and it declared that the overall control was to remain with the Council of Policy, which pleased the Commander.

As time went by, there came a lessening of suspicion between the Dutch and the Huguenots. Gradually, there was a blending of interests through intermarriage and a common bond of economic development. The Drakenstein wine farms established by Huguenot families were often named after familiar landmarks at home in France. The early houses were neither large nor elaborate but, as prosperity grew in the eighteenth century, so did examples of more spacious houses in the inimitable Cape Dutch style. A number of these beautiful white-washed homesteads came to be built in the Drakenstein, of which La Rhône, La Provence and Boschendal are memorable examples. After inspired restoration, on 5 November 1976, Boschendal was declared a national monument.

The expansion of the wine industry became an important economic factor, of benefit both to the Company and the burghers. The arrival of nearly two hundred Huguenots at the Cape was a distinct asset. Many of them had been experienced in the making of wine in France and brought their viticulture skills to an area of South Africa which had a broadly similar climate. Earlier, Simon van der Stel had been the first producer of good wine from Constantia and the two van der Stels, father and son, were leaders in this expanding field. It is noteworthy that a number of the better known examples of present day wineries were in production by 1708, including Constantia and Vergelegen.

More skilled in agricultural pursuits than some of the early Dutch colonists, the Huguenots made a unique contribution to the life of the embryonic Cape colony. Today, the Huguenot Memorial at Franschhoek is an imaginative and fitting tribute to a people whose start in South Africa had begun as the result of a desperate flight from Europe.

CHAPTER 12

Years of Expansion

By 1690, the increased number of European settlers in the Cape had resulted in more land being taken into cultivation "yet the natives were never more friendly." The colonists would have been glad of Khoi labour but a more sedentary life would not have suited a people whose culture rested on a history of stock raising and herding. There was, however, a certain amount of casual labour and the Khoi helped with the harvest in exchange for tobacco and spirits. They would also hire out their daughters as household servants to the Dutch.

The Commander had maintained a good working relationship with Dorha, or Captain Klaas as the Dutch knew him, the captain of a Khoikhoi band through whom a steady supply of cattle was obtained for the fleets. At this time, there were only occasional crimes committed by the Khoi against the settlers. Cattle thefts were not uncommon but more serious offences were unusual. The offenders would be tried by Dutch law and be punished accordingly. In April 1698, a Dutch colonist was murdered by a Khoi at Drakenstein; the culprit was tried and executed. The San or "Bushmen", who had been much in evidence during the earlier European settlement, had largely retreated to the mountains and were too nimble to be caught by Europeans.

Agriculture was by this time sufficiently developed for the Cape to become self-supporting in its foodstuffs for the inhabitants, the garrison and the fleets. In a good year, there was enough wheat for export to Batavia. The Commander, however, made sure that two years' wheat supply was always held in store in case of depredation by drought, caterpillars or locusts. The VOC was increasingly able to rely on the farming of the colonists for the production of crops and stock. It was gradually reducing its own commitments on the grounds of economy. It still had the Company's gardens in Table Valley, the Company's vineyard at Rondebosch, and a number of cattle farms across the country, Hottentots Holland being the most distant. The main emphasis on farm products in order of importance was wheat, cattle and wine. A new farming expansion had taken place in 1687 when a group of burghers moved from Stellenbosch to a site in the Berg River valley, where each had been allocated sixty morgen of land. Later to become an important wine growing area, this expansion marked the siting of Paarl, a new settlement which took its name from a shiny pearl-coloured hill nearby.

From time to time, European politics, particularly those of France, impinged on life at the Cape. In March 1689, it was learned that on 26 November 1688, Louis XIV had declared war against the United Netherlands and had seized all Dutch ships in French ports. The scene was therefore set for possible reprisals at Table Bay and the VOC did not have long to wait. On 26 April 1689, the French ship *Normande* arrived from Pondicherry, well laden with a valuable cargo, and anchored in Table Bay. A boat was sent ashore to convey friendly greetings to the Dutch authorities. As soon as the party reached the castle, they were taken prisoner. The boat was then filled with Dutch sailors in French uniforms who put out from the shore, still flying the French flag. The *Normande* fired a salute during which she was boarded by Dutch crews and a short skirmish ensued in which two Dutch and eight French were wounded, none fatally. The French Captain de Courcelles and his crew surrendered, but it was learned that the *Normande*'s sister ship the *Coche* was not many days behind, so a trap was laid for her by keeping the French flag flying on the *Normande*.

On 5 May, the *Coche* duly approached and anchored in the bay. She gave a nine-gun salute to the Dutch, who replied in the same manner. Nothing more happened for a while, until later in the evening when a boat was sent across to the *Normande*, which did not return. Captain D'Armagnan of the *Coche* became alarmed at midnight when a large Dutch vessel came alongside. He immediately began to prepare the *Coche* for action. The Dutch ship was already prepared and fired a broadside at the *Coche*, killing the captain and three of the crew. The officers on the *Coche* surrendered at once and the Dutch plundered both ships whose cargoes were estimated to have a value of fifty thousand pounds sterling, a vast fortune at the time. The French ships were renamed; the *Normande* became the *Goede Hoop* and the *Coche* became the *Afrika* and they were then sent back to Europe. The one hundred and forty prisoners were sent in the other direction to Batavia.

Although in many respects the Cape economy was buoyant, reports periodically reached the Council of Seventeen that the low salaries which they paid to colonial officials encouraged corruption. As a result of this practice, the Seventeen made a new appointment in the form of an independent fiscal. His job was to scrutinise VOC finances at the Cape and to report any irregularities direct to the Seventeen in Amsterdam. Appointed in 1689, the first holder of this office was Cornelis Simons.

In the year 1691, the Commander was promoted by the Seventeen to the rank of Governor, in recognition of his industrious and capable leadership at the Cape. The following year, a further distinction was accorded him when the Council of Seventeen made him a Councillor Extraordinary of Netherlands India. After twelve years as Commander, Simon van der Stel could look back with pride on a string of imaginative successes. He had opened up new areas of land for cultivation and had greatly improved farming techniques and practices. The immigrants whose establishment he had watched over so carefully had brought much needed new blood to the life of the colony. His close communication with the Seventeen revealed considerable achievement, well beyond their previous expectations. For the most part, the Governor's caring and disciplined approach made him a good diplomat. However, at this time, the Cape inhabitants were becoming increasingly assertive in their appearance and liked to display themselves in more colourful clothes. This caught the Governor's attention and he thought it frivolous and out of keeping with the hard working pioneer image which he sought to maintain. An uncharacteristically puritanical reaction was expressed in a number of decrees, one of which strictly forbade the women of Cape Town to carry sunshades.

The later years of Simon van der Stel's governorship bristled with difficulties. Having built up the Cape economy with flair and imagination, it was quite another task to maintain a balance between conflicting demands and pressures. For a start, there were bitter inter-tribal disputes between two of the more important Khoi chiefs, Captain Klaas, or Dorha, and Captain Koopman. The Governor had had good trading relations with both and it was much in his interests that this useful way of acquiring cattle should be kept open. Klaas had been the favourite but Koopman put about the rumour that Klaas was in a conspiracy against the Company, supported by some groups of disillusioned European settlers. Seized by European troops from the garrison, Klaas was arrested and imprisoned on Robben Island. Koopman then captured the wife of Klaas as part of his plunder. A year later, Klaas was released only to discover that his wife intended to go on living with Koopman. After a further year, she changed her mind again and Koopman murdered her. Supported by his tribesmen, Klaas waged a bitter offensive against Koopman and his tribe, which continued through the remaining years of van der Stel's governorship.

As van Riebeeck had discovered before him, the unquestioning cooperation of the farmers could not be relied upon, which was not entirely their fault. The Council of Seventeen in Amsterdam had laid down strict rules concerning trading arrangements; the burgher farmers found these restricting and would have liked to operate in a freer market with greater rewards for themselves. Van der Stel regularly checked up on a range of routine activities to ensure that they were being properly managed and that all rules were being adhered to. This included waiting until the grapes were ripe before they were picked for wine. One of the reasons for the low quality of Cape wine had been the farmers' unwillingness to let the grapes ripen properly. This surprising shortcoming did not indicate a high degree of intelligence on the part of the farmers, who would be the first to benefit from sales of better wine. Secondly, game was not to be shot without a licence; thirdly, independent direct bartering with the Khoi was not allowed; fourthly, cattle were not to be slaughtered without permits so that a proper check could be kept; and tobacco was not to be imported privately. Furthermore, the Governor's other requirements included the planting of one hundred trees by each farmer who had been established for a minimum of four years. The trees were to be planted on the individual's property and along the Company's roads.

The strict outlook of the Dutch Reformed Church made itself clear in the prohibition of innkeepers to sell drinks during the hours of church services and the forbidding of card games or gambling on Sundays. It was also stipulated that soldiers and sailors were not to be entertained in private houses after sundown; evidently sins of the flesh were anticipated. Stealing produce from the Company's gardens carried the heavy punishment of two years' imprisonment in chains. The ruling concerning fire precautions was of particular importance in the developing town of Cape Town whose buildings were mostly single-storeyed and roofed with thatch. For ease of access, the streets were to be kept clear of wagons and no rubbish or dirt was to be thrown into streets from the adjoining houses.

Particular care was necessary to avoid pollution of the water

FIGURE 14 Cape Colony 1679-1712 From *Historical Atlas of South Africa* by Professor E.A. Walker (courtesy of OUP). Drawn by W. D Howie, as adapted in *The Cape of Good Hope 1652-1833* by G.E. Pearse (courtesy of J.L. Van Schaik, Pretoria).

supply for the castle which came from the spring at the foot of Table Mountain. The water supply was also of vital importance to the ships. For a long while, the manhandling of ships' water casks ashore had proved a cumbersome and inconvenient operation. Simon van der Stel had modernized the whole task by having the water conveyed in pipes for a distance of forty feet out from the edge of Table Bay. The height of the supply pipes above the sea was sufficient for ships' boats to row under the outfall and fill their casks with greater ease. The English clergyman John Ovington recorded his admiration for van der Stel's new system: "The watering of the ships is contrived with such convenience that it is scarce equalled anywhere in the world."

Ovington went on to describe the appearance of Cape Town: "A small town, consisting of about an hundred houses, strong and neatly built with stone walls and pretty apartments." He commented on the leadership of van der Stel in a flowery style: "The present Governor, who lives with his Council in the fort (castle) is a very kind and knowing person, is maintained in grandeur and lives honourably. His public table wants no plenty of European and African wines, or Asian liquors and style, whatever the land or water or air affords in that place, is served up in his bountiful entertainments." Another contemporary visitor, the English traveller, William Dampier, in 1691, described Cape Town: "On the west side of the fort (castle), there is a small Dutch Town, in which I am told there are about fifty or sixty houses; low but well built, with stone walls; there being plenty of stone, drawn out of a quarry close by." However, both travellers complained about the high prices of alcoholic drinks at the local wine house or tavern.

With the growing importance of the castle, a further development of streets took place in the vicinity in 1695. The laying out of the Keizergracht (now Darling Street) completed the area between the Heerengracht (now Adderley Street) and the castle by its westerly-facing entrance.

Peter Kolbe, an educated German, and a tolerable artist, was sent
to the Cape to make astronomical observations. He spent time at
the Cape between 1705 and 1713. Coming later than some of the
other travellers who had commented on the size of Cape Town in
the 1660s, Kolbe was able to appreciate the newer houses. He saw
them as "spacious and built of stone; they have a large court in
front and beautiful gardens behind; and as all show the neatness of
Holland, these buildings present a very beautiful sight. The majority of the houses are of only one storey, none have more than two,
and they are only covered with thatch; one finds a few having a tile
or slate roof, and that because of the boisterous winds which reign
in these parts." He wrote further: "On both sides of the street were
lean-tos to give passers-by shelter from the rain; but they caused
so much inconvenience and danger that they have all been pulled
down by order of the Government. The sailors and Hottentots
were always smoking under these shelters, which caused fires
through their imprudence. The magistrate had to drive them off
the street and prohibit smoking. Those who contravene this regulation are attached to a post and cruelly lashed on the behind." The
severity of this punishment was an indication of the importance
attached to fire precautions, especially in the dry summer season.

One of Simon van der Stel's most effective contributions to the
maintenance of law and order was his setting up of the field cornets or 'veldwagters'. The force was manned by burghers who
were appointed to serve under the 'landdrost' or magistrate for
the area in which they lived. The field cornets thus had a valuable
working knowledge of their locality and its population. One of
their responsibilities was to ensure that every boy who had
reached the age of sixteen joined the burgher militia. They also
acted as surveyors of land and acted in the event of a boundary
dispute between neighbouring farmers. It was considered an honour to serve and, although no salary was paid, field cornets were
exempt from any taxation.

Throughout the early Dutch development of the Cape,

correspondence between the Commander at the Cape and the Council of Seventeen at Amsterdam was prolific. A year might pass before a reply was received but a good insight into the harsh conditions was often provided. Illness and loss of life on the voyage out from the Netherlands was explained in detail by Simon van der Stel in a letter to the Seventeen dated 23 January 1696:

"You mention that you read with great discomposure in our letters of 30 January 1695, the number of deaths on board the outward bound ships and the equally great numbers of sick; and that we are to give you the reasons. This we already did on 9 May last year. The chief causes are the very long voyages by the northern route, and all the accidents met with in consequence, and suffered by the men. Add to this the bad outfit of the sailors, and especially of the soldiers, many of the latter being deserters, and afflicted with army diseases. They are put on board almost unprovided with everything, and become dirty, and wet from bad weather, and rain, and pumping water for the condensers. Having no change, they are obliged to turn in with their wet clothes. This causes a close and stinking atmosphere, to the great injury of the general health. One infects the other, and many, without asking whether their bodies can bear it, go and sleep in the open air during the night. Then there is the unvaried consumption of salt meat and pork, and especially of grey and white peas which are the daily pot food, and by the length of time become musty in the hold – whilst the beer likewise becomes sour. All this old pot food, losing its nourishing qualities and unable to nourish a man in proportion to what he requires, labouring as he does in the heat of the day, finally weakens him so much that he becomes sleepy and lazy, and in the end he gets the scurvy. They lose their appetite, blue knobs and blotches cover the whole body, the gums rot, the patients become shivery and feverish, and fall into fainting fits, from which often dysentery results. They lose heart through want of nourishment, take to their beds, and all germs of strength failing them, they die. This is the unanimous testimony of all the chief surgeons, given by

*order of the Governor, as will be seen from their individual state-
ments. To prevent these diseases as much as possible, good nourishing food is required, and the ships should, better than hitherto, be supplied with barley, plums, raisins, and currants, which,
boiled either with a good dash of rum, and now and then some
Spanish wine, and given to the men morning and evening,
would be wholesome food, whilst the men should always be kept
in a wholesome state of exercise.*

*Regarding the distillation of fresh from sea water, some believe
that the distilled article, having been deprived of its strength is
weak, and will not naturally become cold; others again say that
it is very good and serviceable, and that much depends on good
distillers; the majority agree that it is good for cooking, so that
the ordinary water may be saved, and the men retain their
usual daily allowance."*

Despite an awareness at the Cape of what food made up a good
diet, a sharp criticism was received from Batavia on 1 November
1695 concerning the provisions that had been taken on board by
the *Eyckelenburgh* on her outward voyage. The butler and the cook
had declared that they "had arrived at the Cape from Holland on
7 July, and on 11 October here (at Batavia); that all the preserved
vegetables on board were musty and black, and that the fresh
meat sent on board at the Cape was so old, poor, and unfit to eat
that it could not be boiled, and if roasted, no teeth could bite it
through." They declared that they knew that not only the skipper
and officers, but also many of the men had in consequence
bought many kinds of refreshments from the burghers, including
Cape sheep, carrots, beet, radishes, cabbages, turnips, and salt
fish. They added that they knew that long before the sheep came
on board they had been stabled at the house of the burgher
Schalkwyk in order to learn to eat 'bread' or biscuit, and further,
that all refreshments had been brought on board.

The VOC was always nervous about direct trading between ships' crews and the burghers on account of the financial loss to the Company. The experience of the men of the *Eyckelenburgh*, however, indicated that the VOC itself was not above supplying substandard victuals. The same year, a letter received from the Council of Seventeen in Amsterdam had praised the standard of Cape baking:

> *"As we read that the biscuit baked by you is very good, you are to send us some casks full, to see how it stands the voyage, for if it answers, which we do not doubt, we intend the return fleets to be supplied at the Cape with it, for it is believed that this will tend to the preservation of health, and add to the strength of the men."*

In pursuit of his well-known enthusiasm for planting trees, especially oaks, van der Stel would have been pleased by a letter of 1 August 1696. This was a favourable report from the burgher councillors of the Cape and the 'landdrost' and 'heemraaden' of Stellenbosch and Drakenstein. They had not only been impressed by the Governor during his stay at the Cape speaking of "the necessity of planting forests and other timber." They had also from time to time heard the Governor earnestly advise them to plant, "so that in the course of time this growing colony may not be left in want of fuel and timber." The Governor, however, being a man of action, tended to be exasperated by the more dilatory councillors, who could not be bothered to plant. "Should they delay any longer or refuse, the Governor would have done the work at their cost. In consequence of this order three thousand young oaks have already been planted, and annually more plots will be covered."

Around this time, van der Stel took in hand the question of public security. It was not the first attempt by a Commander of the Cape to do so. A burgher guard was set up "in order to prevent thefts, fights, murders, and other irregularities at night and unseasonable hours in the town and about the castle". The burghers of the Cape district had been ordered to appoint a burgher watch, divided into six companies, so that each would consist of thirty men, who, every afternoon at four o'clock, would come together at their station near the bazaar and mount guard until the morning. They would patrol the whole town, and when they met the military would give a countersign, received every morning from the Governor through a burgher officer.

In a move towards even tighter security, a wider application of countersign was contained in a letter from The Hague, received on 18 May 1695, regarding secret signals for the ships arriving from Holland in case they should be trapped by a foreign presence at the Cape. "As soon as they are within sight or hearing, they shall rapidly fire four guns, and the fort or sailor battery shall reply in the same way with two." This would be a sign that everything at the Cape and Table Bay was in a safe state, and that ships could freely enter. In order to assist in the efficient working of the militia, the farmers, who made up the service, had to keep in touch with each other and within earshot of the signal gun, which might call them to the castle at any time in an emergency.

On 3 May 1697, the Council of Policy passed a resolution to start the construction of a new hospital, to replace the now inadequate hospital of Jan van Riebeeck. It would appear that visiting the sick had more to it than just encouraging the patients, since it was decided: "Henceforth, the Governor and members of the Council, with their wives as outside matrons, should visit the hospital weekly, two and two, in order to prevent or redress all abuses, and look after the comforts of the sick; also seeing that the bedding is kept clean. Eight hundred beds have been provided, stuffed with grass; also a large number of blankets. The grass mattresses can be kept clean better, whilst those stuffed with wool easily breed vermin."

A letter in March 1698 provided a progress report: "The hospital will be completed in four or five months. It is in the form of a cross, 264 feet long and 34 feet broad with the upper storey the same as below. Besides labour, the only extra cost to the Company has been for iron and glass. The old hospital will be used for some other purpose." The progress report, like many others of its kind, was unwisely optimistic. It took nearly two and a half years before the hospital was finished and on 24 October 1699 all the patients from the old hospital were moved to the new one. Several years later, in 1705, the travelling English clergyman, Francis Valentyn, was much impressed by the reputation of the hospital and wrote: "The sick are exceptionally well tended, as appears from the large number who come out cured and continue their journeys whether to India or to the Fatherland."

Early in February 1698, the outward bound fleet brought the news from the Council of Seventeen that Willem Adriaan van der Stel had been appointed Governor in succession to his father, who was due to retire. He was to take on the rank of Governor and Councillor Extraordinary as his father had. Nearly a year after the news of his appointment, Willem Adriaan van der Stel and his family arrived from Holland on 23 January 1699 and he assumed command on 11 February.

Meanwhile, in preparation for the take-over of the governorship by his son, Simon van der Stel had drawn up the customary report of the outgoing Commander for the information and advice of his successor. "It was important," he wrote, "to keep an eye on the farmers and encourage the production of wheat. The cultivation of vineyards must not detract from the growing of wheat, which was the staple food crop." When Simon van der Stel first took over the command, it had been necessary, as we have already seen, to have an annual shipment of rice from Batavia to make up for inadequate wheat harvests at the Cape. By the time of his retirement, the farmers were at last producing enough wheat for their families. Sometimes wheat could even be exported to Batavia in a good year.

Before the end of the seventeenth century, there began a fresh interest in cattle farming, as distinct from crop farming, and in the more flexible way of life that went with it. This development led to the spread of the 'trekboer' movement in search of new pastures further away from the south-west Cape lowlands and into new areas east of the barrier of the Hottentots Holland mountains. The natural geographical boundary was traversed in particular by a pass near the southern end, later to become known as Sir Lowry's pass. In order not to conflict with the Company interests, it was important that the 'trekkers' or farmers did not spread their wagons at the Company's outposts, nor use the Company's grazing and water. Among the grazing, there had been an unwelcome tendency for farmers to let their stock run with the Company's, to the detriment of the Company's grazing provision.

The Company's servants had been encouraged to become freemen so that others would follow them from Holland and from the Indies. It was considered important that they should be Dutch and Protestant, or German and Protestant. Always suspicious of the French, the Governor had even feared the possibility of civil war. He wrote to his son, "the French nation, though settled here and well received, are the least to be trusted."

A note of patriotism came in his advice to his son: "Above all avoid adventurers, fortune-hunters, people who come to make what they can out of the country and then clear out with their profits. Such people should be taxed when they leave, then the country that served them would have some reward for its hospitality." With regard to the Khoi, he advised "govern them with great gentleness. We have accustomed them not to make war upon one another. They come to us to be reconciled." Such had not always been the case and the improvement in relations was to be welcomed.

In the lengthy document to his son, the economics of timber

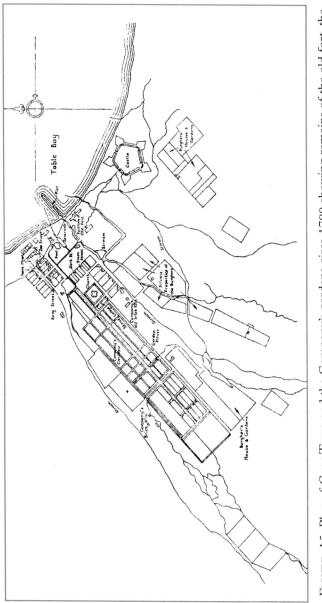

FIGURE 15 Plan of Cape Town and the Company's gardens circa 1700 showing remains of the old fort, the new fort (castle), slave quarters (slave lodge), water courses and other features. Adapted from *The Cape of Good Hope 1652–1833* by G.E. Pearse, 1956 (courtesy of J.L. Van Schaik, Pretoria).

production and transport characteristically found a place. More and more timber trees needed to be planted and roads would be needed for the forests around Hottentots Holland. Oxen were too slow for the quickening pace of life and there was a need to breed more horses. The retiring Governor ended with a fulsome blessing on his son's future responsibilities. Very different from the way events turned out, it reflected a devotion and admiration of father to son and a glowing future. "We commend you and the Company's possessions to the Holy and Worthy Protection of the Almighty, cordially praying His Divine Majesty to guide you with His Holy Spirit, and grant you such prudence and justice, and likewise such an upright, pure and steadfast mind, combined with such faithful diligence as you may be in need for the administration of Church and State, and the furtherance of the Company's interests here, that your work may tend to magnify God's Holy Name, satisfy our masters, and preserve and increase your own honour and reputation."

Unlike his predecessors, Simon van der Stel had no wish to spend his retirement in Holland and he retired to his elegant house at Groot Constantia, surrounded by its oak avenues and sheltered farmland in the Cape peninsula. At Constantia, he continued to entertain generously and his appreciative guests found the fish, game and meat unsurpassed. Guests would come and stay and were full of admiration for their host. The retired Governor enjoyed an active way of life among his vineyards and cattle pastures. He looked after his employees well, giving them good working conditions and wages. In the space of ten years, a wide variety of fruit trees was planted, including mulberries, lemons, limes, quinces, apricots, peaches, almonds, pomegranates and pears. The list represented a mixture of cool temperate and warm temperate fruits.

In March 1699, the visiting Commissioner granted Simon van der Stel an enlargement of his property with the addition of neighbouring lands at Zeekoe Vlie. A further addition was granted by the Commissioner who came in February 1700, when the grazing lands of Steenberg Tokai were given to him for his life-time.

Simon van der Stel holds a unique place in the history of South Africa. His creativity and leadership were unrivalled by any other Governor of the Cape; his loyalty and enthusiasm sprang from a devotion to his work to the last. He died at his much loved Constantia on 24 June 1712 at the age of 73 and was buried at the new church in Cape Town. It was a fitting South African tribute to him that the Simon van der Stel Foundation, the important national preservation society, was formed in 1959.

CHAPTER 13

Willem Adriaan's Misjudgments

Born in 1664, Willem Adriaan van der Stel went to the Cape with his family in 1679. At the age of twenty, he returned to Amsterdam in 1684 and worked for the VOC. He subsequently married Maria de Hase and they raised a family of six children, three daughters and three sons.

His installation as Governor on 11 February 1699 was marked by a great parade of garrison men and the militia. Celebrations in honour of the occasion included the pardoning of imprisoned runaway servants of the VOC, and the release from chains of convicts who had been fettered.

A population census at the time of the change of governors listed: four hundred and fourteen freemen, two hundred and seven women, two hundred and fifty five boys, and two hundred and sixty six girls. Burgher slaves totalled five hundred and thirty six men, eighty four women, twenty nine boys, and twenty eight girls. The figures indicated a satisfactory growth in the Cape community overall, although the dependence on slaves was high.

Willem Adriaan van der Stel was something of an enigma. He had been a magistrate in Amsterdam at the heart of the VOC operations. When his appointment to the Cape in succession to his father was made known, he was congratulated by the member chambers of the Company. The Chamber of Hoorn was delighted and wrote to say that it was "an appointment that greatly pleased this Chamber." Soon after his arrival at the Cape, an account of personal expenses threw a singular light on Willem

Adriaan's tastes and predilections. In 1701, there were entries for "wine from Mainz, Germany, three grey wigs of differing complexity, scented oils and powders". The following year, he ordered glass rummers and violin strings.

On a more practical note, the new Governor had inherited his father's interest and skills in gardens and tree planting and Willem Adriaan spent a very constructive first year in office. On the day after his arrival, he was on the pier to supervise the unloading of boxes containing young trees, mainly oaks and other plants from Holland. They were conveyed to the Company's gardens. He inspected forests and planted some thirty thousand oaks. The people of Stellenbosch were to collect twelve thousand oaks to plant around the settlement, of which eight thousand were destined for Drakenstein. To the Company's garden in Cape Town, the new Governor added a natural history museum and a small zoological garden.

Nine months after taking over the Cape administration, Willem Adriaan set out on a tour of inspection of the colony and its outposts. The tour included a visit to the outlying farms in addition to the settlements of Drakenstein, Stellenbosch and Tigerberg. Going further inland than any governor had done previously, he followed the upper section of the Klein Berg River through the Obiqua range. On the further side he found a region of great variety enclosed by mountains on three sides: west, north and east. The profusion of natural grassland in what struck Willem Adriaan as an area of great beauty would be ideal for stock grazing. The abundance of natural forest on the mountain slopes would provide a good source of timber. He named this paradise the Land of Waveren after his great-grandmother whose surname was Waveren. Within a year, the first settlers had moved in with their cattle to take advantage of this discovery on the pioneer fringe of the south western Cape lowlands. The Land of Waveren, later to be known as the Tulbagh Basin, was well situated for one of the natural routes leading up to the Karoo through the Hex River valley. In more modern times, this route has been followed by the railway line from Cape Town to Johannesburg, and by improved roads.

The importance of cattle breeding by the Europeans was growing as a result of failing trade with the Khoi. The gradual disintegration of the tribes made for an uncertain meat trade, and the new Governor needed to introduce fresh pastures on which cattle and sheep might be reared. Shortly after the Governor's tour, Henning Huising, the burgher farmer and butcher had his meat contract with the Company renewed for the supply of beef and mutton at a fixed price. Experience had shown that Huising was not only a shrewd businessman but also skilled at fattening up and greatly improving indifferent stock.

Early in 1700, the first new areas of pasture to be used were those at Riebeeck's Kasteel and a few months later a group of new arrivals from Europe set up the first cattle farms in the Land of Waveren, around Tulbagh in the north eastern corner. These developments on the initiative of the Governor provided some extra space for which the burghers had been insistently asking.

In 1701, the easterly spread into new country brought the graziers into conflict with the San people or 'Bushmen'. An early example of this was the invading of a European cattle farm at Riebeeck's Kasteel when a large number of cattle was taken. The Governor speedily arranged for the dispatch of soldiers to guard the new areas but they were not successful in warding off the San people. Alarm spread through the farmers when more than one hundred cattle were seized by a seemingly irrepressible group. Fear was not peculiar to the Europeans; the Khoi cattle owners became involved too and shared in the general alarm. One of the European farmers, Gerrit Cloete, who had suffered most at the hands of the thieving San, together with Captain Klaas of the Khoi mounted a joint defence force and search campaign in the absence of any effective action on the part of the military. Many

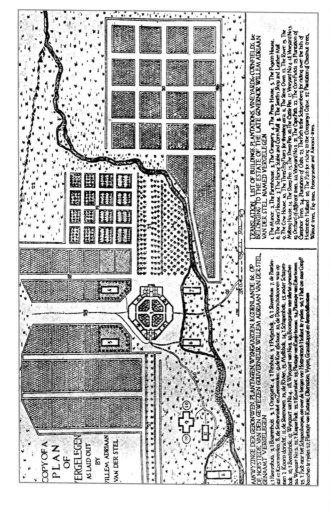

FIGURE 16 Plan of Vergelegen as laid out by Willem Adriaan van der Stel. From *Historic Houses of South Africa* by Dorothea Fairbridge (1922) (courtesy of OUP, as adapted in *The Cape of Good Hope 1652-1833* by G.E. Pearse, courtesy of J.L.Van Schaik, Pretoria).

forays took place between the soldiers and the Khoi during the next year. Eventually, the threat from the Khoi receded but it was necessary to keep up a military presence in order to protect the farmers and their stock.

By the time of the younger van der Stel's accession, relations between the Dutch settlers and the French Huguenots had become warmer; earlier animosities were dying out. The French pastor, Pierre Simond, was responsible for the community at Drakenstein where the prominent hill, known as Simondium, had been named after him. The pastoral vacancy at Stellenbosch was filled in 1700 by the Dutch minister Herculese van Loon. Unfortunately, all did not go well with him and, after a ministry of only four months, he committed suicide.

With the increasing popularity of cattle farming which had become apparent in the later years of Simon van der Stel's governorship, his son had to face sharply increased demands for independence from VOC restrictions and freedom to trek inland through the mountain ranges that hitherto had put a physical boundary on the eastern edge of the European settlement.

The possibility of building a new church in the centre of Cape Town had been under discussion for some years owing to the growing inadequacy of the small church within the castle precincts, which had been extensively used as a burial ground. With plans completed several years before, the Governor laid the foundation stone for the new church at the end of December 1700. The church occupied a site at the northern end of the Company's gardens where the Groote Kerke now stands; the first service in the new church was held in January 1704. The English traveller Valentyn visited the church in 1714, ten years after its completion. He recorded its octagonal shape and four circular whitewashed columns supporting the roof. He found the church to be "fifty paces along," and not surprisingly in view of its plan, fifty paces wide. A separate cemetery was established.

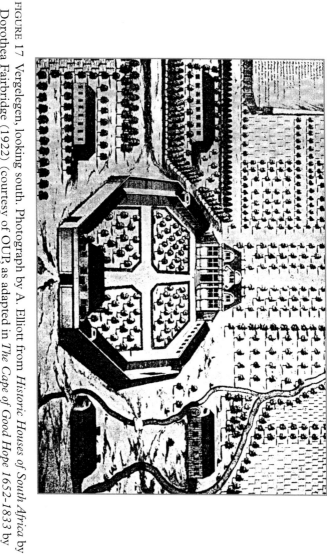

FIGURE 17 Vergelegen, looking south. Photograph by A. Elliott from *Historic Houses of South Africa* by Dorothea Fairbridge (1922) (courtesy of OUP, as adapted in *The Cape of Good Hope 1652-1833* by G.E. Pearse, courtesy of J.L. Van Schaik, Pretoria).

After his arrival at the Cape, Willem Adriaan van der Stel lost no time in making his mark on the landscape. In 1700, the VOC visiting Commissioner Wouter Valkenir granted him a holding of 400 morgen (over 800 acres) of land on the Lourens River, close to the north-east corner of False Bay. It was a beautiful lush setting in a well-watered landscape surrounded on three sides by the spectacularly blue Hottentots Holland mountains. The Governor named his property in this lovely area Vergelegen. It became a lavish establishment from which Willem Adriaan supervised his growing estate. The house formed one side of an octagonal walled enclosure within which a formal garden was created. The main elevation of the house was approached by a carefully laid out avenue of oaks. The inspiration for this estate would certainly have come in part from his father's property at Groot Constantia, in the Cape Peninsula.

Willem Adriaan was, like his father, a patron of architecture and both van der Stels led the way in the design and construction of the earliest Cape Dutch homesteads. These houses were able to enjoy a spaciousness in the landscape of the Cape unknown in the Netherlands. The van der Stels themselves, father and son, enriched the setting of their houses by planting avenues of oak trees. At Vergelegen, some camphor trees planted by Willem Adriaan are still standing and noted for their great size. Typical features of both Groot Constantia and Vergelegen as they later developed were the whitewashed exteriors, a low terrace or 'stoep' where the household might gather, and a thatched roof with a decorative gable in the centre. In the Netherlands, the gable would usually form part of the narrow end wall, which contained the main entrance overlooking the street or canal. In the Cape landscape, there were no such restrictions on space and it became the custom to make the gable the chief ornament of the long facade.

Territorially, Henning Huising ranked close to the van der Stels and, like them, he was an early builder of a homestead in the early

Cape Dutch style at Meerlust. Patronage in architecture, financed by the proceeds of acquired affluence through trade, has many examples around the world. Its emergence in this unique way in South Africa is a telling reminder of the gradual spread of wealth which was just becoming apparent by 1700 and which blossomed as the eighteenth century unfolded.

The Governor was a highly competent farmer and administrator, with a strong motive for personal gain. It was not long before other VOC officials set up their own farms, including Samuel Elsevier, the secunde or second in command, who owned 110 morgen; Captain Olof Berg, the officer in command, owned 297 morgen; Johan Blesius, the fiscal, owned 120 morgen; Petrus Kalden, the clergyman, owned at least 100 morgen; and William ten Damme, the surgeon, at least 60 morgen.

Having received the original grant of 400 morgen, the Governor then set about extending this allocation by making grants to others and leasing back the land to himself. By this dubious means he obtained a total area of 613 morgen (well over 1200 acres). Together with the other officials who had taken on land, the Governor could easily supply the whole Cape market without the need to buy the produce of the ordinary farmers. As a result the ordinary farmers found that their market outlets, by virtue of the competition from the Governor and his friends, were either greatly reduced or stopped altogether. A private cartel was thus created within the VOC trading monopoly and the Governor began to be very unpopular with the farmers.

From the start, Willem Adriaan had set about developing his land in a vigorous and ruthless way. He removed quantities of the best plants from the Company's garden and dispatched the Company's master gardener, Jan Hertog, to lay out his own grounds at Vergelegen. Using a large labour force of sixty Europeans and a great many slaves, diverted from their customary tasks with the VOC at the Cape, the Governor set about converting his land for the cultivation of vines and grain in particular. Great gangs of slaves and a large number of soldiers and convalescent sailors, who were skilful agriculturists or mechanics, were constantly at work there until the farm, which had been expanded to 613 morgen, assumed the appearance of the most highly cultivated ground in South Africa. The Governor also made use of three old VOC stations in Hottentots Holland, two of them for cattle pasture and one at Vishoek which had been well equipped for fishing.

In these circumstances, it was hardly surprising that the English traveller John Maxwell, who visited the Company's garden in 1708, portrayed in a letter an impression of reduced standards: "The Company's garden is not now in the fine order it was in during this governor's father's time, when it was divided into four parts, in each of which grew an abundance of the more remarkable vegetables belonging to its corresponding quarter of the world, but tho' the climate, soil, and situation are very favourable, 'tis now much neglected both in respect of its plants and walks, neither of which are extraordinary."

Willem Adriaan van der Stel was, like his father, skilled in viticulture. At Vergelegen, he planted vine stocks as a major component of his farming policy. He admitted to planting two hundred thousand vines but the farmers declared that four hundred thousand was a truer figure. He planted his stocks more widely spaced than did the ordinary farmer, which produced a better growth. On the 61 morgen planted with vines, there would have been at least five hundred thousand vine stocks. The Governor was adamant that he owned 400 morgen of land but the land registers, a part of the VOC documentation, proved that the correct figure was 613 morgen. He declared that he had over two hundred and fifty people working for him but the farmers reckoned that a workforce of three hundred and fifty was the more accurate figure. VOC records indicated that his own figures were clearly an underestimation.

When the farmers began their campaign against the Governor, they sought to prove that his farming operations were strongly against those of the ordinary burghers whose very livelihood was at stake. The Governor was the first to set up grazing stations beyond the Cape lowlands and he had eighteen of them beyond the route through Hottentots Holland mountains, later named Sir Lowry's pass. At his instigation, eighteen thousand sheep and one thousand cattle were raised beyond the pass in what later became a trekking area near Caledon.

Although in retirement as Governor, Simon van der Stel continued to be an active landowner and was the second largest farmer after his son Willem Adriaan. Apart from his cultivated land at Groot Constantia, he had a large area of pastureland for cattle raising, which extended as far south as Simonstown, another settlement named after himself. Willem Adriaan's younger brother Frans was also a farming landowner at Parelvallei in Hottentots Holland and he had a cattle station at Riebeeck's Kasteel. Between them, the two brothers virtually monopolized the farming of the very fertile Hottentots Holland district.

The van der Stel family taken together with the other landowning officials were reckoned to have had between them as much farmland as two hundred ordinary farmers. In 1705, it was estimated that there were four hundred farmers who owned land, in which case the Governor and his particular group were responsible for one half of all the farming land in the Cape colony. Unlike the ordinary farmer, they paid no tithe and could therefore conceal high production figures and their leading share of the market.

The observant traveller Valentyn made a visit to Vergelegen with Willem Adriaan in 1705. He recorded his impression in his journal: "We left Cape Town at six in the evening in a coach with six horses and reached Vergelegen at twelve, having changed horses once along the road. The next day I saw the beautiful home which is surrounded by a thick, high, ornamented octagonal wall to keep out the wild animals. The hall in the centre of the house was eighty feet long and sixteen feet wide. Fine views are obtained from one side across False Bay to the mountains, vineyards and other lands. On the other side is a flower garden and a fine river with two branches. On both sides of this well-lit and lofty hall are four beautiful apartments, and next to these on either side are four more, very beautifully furnished and worthy, and because of their beauty and costliness have been spared by the Council of Seventeen which had the rest of the house broken down." It is not difficult to imagine the irritation of the Seventeen at the extravagance of one of their senior employees.

The political scene was increasingly dominated by the growing discontent of the Cape burghers. The Governor appeared to be intransigent in his dealings with them and was a difficult man to approach. Willem Adriaan was himself a highly competent entrepreneur and successful trader, and less distinguished mortals envied him. However, he lacked the diplomatic manner of his father and was less than caring in the way he handled the disenchanted burghers. He did, however, set about improving the conditions of the colony and relations with the Khoi. The Namaqua peoples, with whom his father had had good connections on his expedition to Namaqualand a few years previously, remained friendly and in 1705 an alliance was formed. A number of leading Namaquas then paid visits to the castle where they were warmly entertained by the Governor and had gifts showered upon them. Each chief was given a copper-headed staff as a token of his chieftainship and recognition by the Governor, a repetition of the gifts made by Commander Isbrand Goske to Captains Klaas and Koopman some years before.

Although Willem Adriaan's afforestation plans were in hand, the shortage of timber led him to seek other possible supplies further away. He turned his attention to Natal, where he believed there to be a good coverage of natural timber readily accessible to the sea. In search of this, the *Postlooper* sailed from Table Bay towards the

FIGURE 18 View of Cape Town harbour with water-battery.
Seen from the south west, c. 1762. (Permission from the National Library of South Africa).

end of 1705. The captain was given the naive instruction to confirm the ownership of a strip of Natal purchased some twenty years earlier from a local chief, whose successor made it plain to the captain that he knew nothing of any such transaction, nor would he regard it as valid. The *Postlooper* then returned to Cape Town empty handed as far as new timber resources were concerned.

Among the more trivial aspects of indiscipline, and apparent lack of respect for the Governor, was the attitude of the free burgher, Jan Rotterdam. This citizen made a point of remaining seated in church and did not stand up on the entry of the Governor. The Council of Policy investigated this as a presumed slight and reported that when in church Rotterdam was only too glad if he could quickly reach his seat in order to sit down, for a singular reason. If he stood up, "he begged pardon," he "wetted his trousers in consequence of a certain disease," which had kept him more than a year from church. Rotterdam said he intended no disrespect towards the Governor, "but on account of the disease mentioned, he had always remained sitting and dared not stand up." It was later discovered that he was a fraud and that there was nothing physically the matter with him. The authorities were infuriated at having their time wasted by such an enquiry when there were many other demands on their attention.

Of a more serious nature, one of the major irritations of which the populace repeatedly complained was the preemption of markets by the Governor to their detriment and his profit. In particular, the high productivity of fruit and wine swamped the market outlets, which were not large enough to take both the Governor's high pressure economics and the more desultory output of the ordinary burghers. The amount of land granted to the Governor was held to be excessive. However, the efficient way in which he organised his workforce without doubt made his own farming enterprise the source of much comment among the burghers.

So intent was the Governor on his new works at Vergelegen that he neglected his responsibilities at the castle, although he could be there at short notice on horseback if anything untoward occurred. The Netherlands were then involved in the war of Spanish Succession which was waged from 1701 to 1714, and it was quite possible that the French might attack the Cape to intercept the richly laden VOC ships from the east. Fortunately, this never happened but no credit was due to the Governor whose chief concern was to gather in funds for his own advantage at the expense of the livelihood of the burghers.

Apart from the victualling of ships, which had been the main purpose of the original Dutch settlement, the Cape market was a small one chiefly concerned with the three commodities of wheat, meat and wine. At the end of the seventeenth century, the VOC gave up their direct interest in production and let the burghers carry it on individually.

In addition to wine and fruit, the Governor's farm also produced wheat. It was soon alleged that he produced nearly one quarter of the output of the Cape colony to the detriment of the ordinary farmers. It must be remembered, however, that wheat cultivation was now thought by some to be a tedious occupation and less agreeable than cattle raising. With typical van der Stel determination, it would not have been difficult for him to take the lead in the output of wheat. He contrived to benefit through the use of a new franchise determined at the annual auction. Grain was normally produced for local consumption and corn mills were set up on the larger estates such as Vergelegen. In a good year, there would even be a surplus for export to Batavia.

The meat trade remained in the competent hands of Henning Huising until the Governor transferred control of it after an event in 1702, when a party of burghers engaged in a bartering mission with some Khoi found themselves being attacked. In return, they had plundered the Khoi and behaved in an uncivilised manner.

The Governor seized this opportunity to suspend the free barter between the burghers and the Khoi. This suspension by the Governor of an authorised policy ought first to have been sanctioned by the Council of Seventeen, but he took it upon himself to make the decision. In place of the previous system, he appointed four slaughterers of his own choosing in the knowledge that they would be amenable to his way of charging which Huising was not.

The Governor also began to work out the best way of securing for himself a goodly profit from the wine trade. After many years of very indifferent wine at the Cape, the Governor's father had raised the standard, as indeed had the expertise of the Huguenot settlers from France. By the time Willem Adriaan van der Stel was in business, the standard of Cape wine had been much improved. In conjunction with some other officials, he used the annual auction of 1705 as the occasion on which to change the rules. Instead of having four concessionaires for wine distribution, as had been the custom, he made it possible for a single concessionaire to win the whole lot. A supporter of his, Johannes Phijffer, was the chosen man for this scheme. At the auction, the new conditions were read out, to the amazement of those who had expected to hear the usual formula. It became all too apparent that the Governor planned to arrange the distribution of wine sales in a way that would be of financial benefit to himself and spell ruin to the wine farmers.

At first the burghers merely complained among themselves, but after a while they became more organised. Both Dutch and Huguenot farmers, with their very different backgrounds, shared a common belief that they were being put upon. In 1705 farmers from both groups decided jointly on a course of action. A secret meeting took place at which a list of charges against the Governor was put together and then sent to Batavia. If this was the start of a movement, it was clear that someone to coordinate it would be needed. Such a person came forward in the form of Adam Tas.

CHAPTER 14

Downfall of Willem Adriaan

Adam Tas was born in Amsterdam in 1688, and had, coinciden-tally, an early link with the Cape. His maternal aunt, Maria Lindenhovius, had been a domestic servant in the household of Simon van der Stel. From his house, she had married Henning Huising, who later became the most influential burgher farmer at the Cape. He was well thought of, in particular through his enter-prising trade in meat.

With the background of this family connection, Adam Tas jour-neyed to the Cape in 1697 and was employed by his uncle in a secretarial capacity. In 1699, he was commissioned as ensign in the burgher militia, which suggested that he had acquired some degree of standing in the community. However, even before seri-ous animosity took over, the Governor looked on him as an idle fellow, who would "go lounging up and down, and every day about the neighbourhood be wagging a forward tongue." It has to be said that this impression was also gained from reading the pub-lished version of Adam Tas's own diary. In June 1703, Adam Tas married a rich farmer's widow, Elizabeth van Brakel, and thereby moved into a more affluent way of life. The Governor was moved to comment: "within this glassy clover meadow this canting rogue, that with padding of the streets, and with those many years of idle living, was come by no great profit, did attain unto an ease-ful, fortunate, and right pleasant estate."

Adam Tas drew up a petition for the Council of Seventeen in Amsterdam detailing allegations of wrong practice by the Governor. A large gathering of disgruntled burghers met at

Henning Huising's house and arising out of this meeting over sixty signatures were collected for the petition. Criticism of the Governor's personal behaviour continued to grow and on Christmas Eve in 1705 Adam Tas recorded in his diary that the Governor's wife had tried to drown herself in the fountain behind their house. She had been rescued by the wife of Berg, the army commander, to whom she had confessed that her life had become one of terror on account of the many scandalous acts she must daily hear and witness. Possibly not unrelated to this comment, some while later, the Governor forbade the reading of the Ten Commandments when he came to church, presumably since he knew he had broken so many of them. Even allowing for exaggeration by a writer who had a low opinion of the Governor, the two reported events have a ring of truth about them.

Two months later, only a week before Adam Tas was taken into custody, his diary went into some detail with regard to the relationship between the burghers and the Governor at this time of uncertain loyalties, when the latter was attempting to gain their support. The entry in Tas's diary for Sunday, 20 February 1706 provided graphic details:

> *"Fair morning. This morning I rode to Mr du Toit's in company with Mr van der Bijl, but found him not at home, as he had been bidden to the home of Matthijs Greef, so we rode thither. Mr Appel also came thither, where we were told that yesterday all the free burghers at the Cape, including some blacks, were summoned by the officer to the presence of the Governor. Having arrived in the castle, they were treated with wine, tobacco, etc. The Governor next produced a document, which he made them sign. The people were amazed, not knowing what this meant, yet not daring to set their hand to it. This shall embody a declaration that they esteem the Governor for an honest man. Yet they are rogues who do such a thing, unless it be people who have found the Governor's lost honour, for so it would be but fair if they return it to him, but in my view the pitiable figure, which*

the Governor cuts at present, are nothing but his last convul-
sions. Mr Greef was merry, loudly singing several tunes, but he
was full with sweet wine. He declared that he would rather lose
his head than sign for the Governor, and he made out such as
signed for the Governor to be accursed rogues, and went so far
that he would wish them damned in hell. After we had spent
some time there, drunk sundry glasses of wine and burned some
tobacco, we rode to the house of Mr du Toit, where we had din-
ner, and then rode home. This night we heard loud knocking on
the door, the caller being Abraham Bleusel, who had come riding
from Drakenstein (true heart) to tell me how he and some fifteen
other Frenchmen had been to the house of François du Toit,
where the landdrost wanted them to sign a document in favour
of the Governor. First the landdrost tried to induce them by
promises, and afterwards with fierce threats.

During this time he was so overcome with wrath that he became
livid in the face and was shaking as he read out the document.
A ruffian stood guard at the door, which he had locked.
Abraham Bleusel started speaking and roundly declared that
he had a mind to sign, but first wanted to set out his grievances
above it, and if he might not do that, he would not sign. After
this man had spoken, the people, who had gathered there, went
their ways without anyone consenting to sign, so that the land-
drost came away empty handed, his threats having availed him
nothing. I hope that the pestilent rogue will fare likewise in
other places. After this man had finished telling his tale, and
had drunk a glass or two of wine, he took horse again and rode
to Drakenstein."

Adam Tas and his supporters were determined to carry on with
their petition. However, when the Governor realized that a petition was being collected for the Seventeen, he was determined to
have it stopped at all costs. Acting on the Governor's orders,
the landdrost of Stellenbosch went to Adam Tas's farm on
28 February 1706 and arrested him.

Not all the faults were Willem Adriaan's. Adam Tas had drawn up a plan of Vergelegen emphasising the allegedly grandiose nature of the Governor's country house. However, he was forced to admit that he had never been to Vergelegen and that his drawing was imaginary. Tas was taken to the castle and put in gaol where he was held for over a year. His house was closely searched; a rough draft of the petition was discovered in his writing desk. The final copy not being found, Willem Adriaan was left wondering whether it had gone to Amsterdam.

A few days after the arrest, the Council of Policy prescribed heavy penalties for any colonists who put their names to "malicious" documents critical of the Governor. Several arrests were made among Adam Tas's chief supporters. Jacob van der Heiden, who had been a longstanding friend, and Wessel Pretorius were also imprisoned in Cape Town. Henning Huising, who had been a friend and supporter of both van der Stels, was held prisoner awaiting trial. He was one of four prisoners who claimed the right to be tried before a court in the Netherlands. It was held that a case involving prominent burghers in conflict with the Governor was too big to be handled by the Court of Justice at the Cape. The Governor was, understandably, anxious that the trial should not achieve the status attaching to a court in Holland, but the Broad Council decided otherwise and upheld the prisoners' claim. The homeward bound fleet called at Table Bay at the end of March. Henning Huising and three other prisoners were taken aboard one of the ships and sailed to Holland on 4 April 1706. With them went the petition which the Governor had been anxious to retrieve.

Meanwhile at the Cape there was disorder and confusion and a good deal of ill-feeling. Some of the more eccentric members of the community took advantage of the situation and behaved in a riotous manner. The Reverend Egbertus Le Bourcq was seen riding, running and trotting about dangerously, armed with a sword and two pistols, evidently uncertain as to which weapon he might use first. Relations between the Governor and the burghers were at a low ebb. They were not improved by van der Stel discovering that some people were still making trouble against him. Summoned to appear in court on charges of sedition, the colonists failed to appear and, in their absence, they were banished from the colony. This presupposed that the men could be found and their sentences implemented. The rebel burghers remained undeterred.

Later in the year, in September 1706, a group of farmers defiantly paraded in Stellenbosch and beat a drum outside the landdrost's office. The landdrost's order to desist was ignored and dancing took place. There was an outbreak of similar incidents in opposition to the Government. In an attempt to rescue some semblance of law and order, a body of soldiers came after nightfall later in the month to round up the culprits. However, news of the plan had leaked in advance and no-one could be found. The Landdrost Starrenberg and his supporting militia had a difficult task in the face of passive non-cooperation from the burgher community. Six months later, by March 1707, the Governor had eventually tracked down many of the rebels but it was not a cause for triumph since much constitutional damage had been done.

In the following month, news reached the Cape concerning the response of the Council of Seventeen to Adam Tas's petition. After receiving the petition, the Seventeen had appointed a special Commission at the Cape to study the criticisms contained in the burghers' document. The Council's reply, dated 30 October 1706, started on a somewhat dismissive note:

> "Letters received on 27 July, dated 31 March. They contain the, to us, unpalatable news of excessive commotions and quarrels between a large portion of the colonists and the Cape Government, with whose charges and counter-charges a large quantity of paper has been covered, greatly to the hindrance of our business, and at the same time causing us no end of trouble.

For the present we will say nothing more of the whole affair, than that we expect for the future such and similar distasteful subjects will not be placed before us by either side, but that everyone, satisfying himself with what he may fairly claim, will remain quiet and in peace, and refrain from complaints."

However, the report went on to criticise strongly the behaviour of the Governor and his chief supporters and to deliver the astounding order:

"We have, for the sake of maintaining the general peace in this colony, and for other valid reasons, decided that from it shall be removed and sent hither the Governor Willem Adriaan van der Stel, the second person Samuel Elsevier, the Minister Petrus Kalden, and the Landdrost Johannes Starrenburgh, with the retention of their pay and rank, but without retaining any authority or command, and that if possible they are to leave with the first return ships expected here in 1707."

It was in April 1707 that this news reached the Cape. Those who had been imprisoned were to be released at once, including Adam Tas. The Cape burghers were delighted but Willem Adriaan van der Stel was shocked and highly embarrassed by the situation in which he found himself.

On the question of the large scale nature of the 400 morgen (over 800 acres) estate at Vergelegen that had been granted to Willem Adriaan in 1700 as his own property by the Ordinary Councillor Wouter Valkenier, the Seventeen complained that they had not been fully informed. "Much less has our approval of it been asked or given." The Seventeen now required the property to be restored to the Company, including the whole plantation. "Regarding the homestead with its buildings, stables, slave quarters, etc. it is suggested that a price be agreed with Willem Adriaan and that it should be taken over for the Company." The Company, however, would have nothing to do with the dwelling house, "which we desire shall be broken down by him, as such buildings which are for ostentation and more for pomp than use have been built by the Company's servants at the Cape and elsewhere in India greatly to our annoyance, and in a very prominent fashion." On learning the news from Amsterdam, the first reaction of the deposed Governor was to play for time. He busied himself with work on his estate at Vergelegen, which he had no wish to leave.

A letter to the Seventeen dated 24 December 1707 from the Commission at the Cape reported van der Stel's complaints against the harshness of the proceedings which, he submitted, had been taken against him. He strongly protested against the resolution, which had been not only read to him but of which he had also been handed a copy:

> "And whereas we have been informed that the said Mr van der Stel, after he had been informed of the decision of the Directors, had the lands ploughed and sown with large quantities of grain, etc. He declared that the land had been ploughed and sown, and that the largest portion of the seed had been put in before your orders had been received; and further, being in that great trouble, he had remained here at the Cape, without thinking of the requirements of his lands; that in the meanwhile his men and servants had continued sowing, just as they had always been accustomed to do; and that at the same time nothing had been said about it and he had likewise not been forbidden to do so."

With no time limit set, van der Stel urgently requested the Council of Seventeen to cancel the resolution. He protested that since he was drawing no salary nor rations, he would not be able to pay the workforce wages.

The Cape Council held to its resolution. "We are decided not to allow Mr van der Stel to postpone everything until your reply had been received. Mr Van der Stel is still in possession of the farm

Vergelegen without making any signs of removing thence with his people and goods." A number of Commissioners visited Willem Adriaan and told him to leave the Cape by the end of January 1708.

When on 31 December 1707, the Commissioners saw Willem Adriaan, he insisted that he wanted to verify the ownership of the grain about to be harvested. He further wished his removal time to be extended from 31 January to the end of February when he would be sufficiently prepared to carry out the resolution of the Council. On 10 January, the Commissioners decided to let van der Stel reap all the corn at Vergelegen for his own benefit, on condition of his paying the tithes to the Company. This he did, with the understanding that if their decision was disapproved by the Council of Seventeen, he would be bound to pay the value back in money.

On 17 February 1708, the Commissioners wrote to the Council of Seventeen to confirm that not only January had passed but a large part of February likewise and, although Mr van der Stel had asked to stay on for two or three weeks longer, he had not yet made any preparations to leave the place. Still more reasons for prevarication were produced by the wily ex-Governor. The approaching vintage was held to be a cause for concern and the need to reach an agreement with the Council of Seventeen was a new factor. Willem Adriaan was to use his own materials and casks for pressing the grapes and the Commissioners were to be present on behalf of the Company to record quantities and types. This followed the arrival of an increasingly impatient letter from the Seventeen which had been written on 2 October 1707: "In reply to your letter of 15 April, with a PS of 25, we beg to say that it appears strange to us that the late Governor Willem Adriaan van der Stel requests that he may remain at the Cape as a forgotten burgher, which we by no means allow. On the contrary it is our express order that he shall come over at once." Moreover, in the absence of cooperation, his salary would be cut off.

While the different problems related to the recall of Willem Adriaan van der Stel were being resolved, the new Governor, Louis van Assenburgh, had arrived at the Cape on 25 January 1708 and was installed on 1 February. A friendly message of goodwill was received from Jan Rotterdam, the free burgher who had earlier caused trouble: "Van Assenburgh congratulated. The wish is expressed that he may retain the appointment for many years to the contentment of the people and the prosperity of the Company." A week after van Assenburgh's installation, a more personal greeting was sent to him from Robben Island: "The Superintendent congratulates Governor van Assenburgh on his safe arrival from Europe. After twenty four years' service here, he has the honour of congratulating Mr van Assenburgh as his third Governor during that time. May God grant you a long and continuing health, so that you may be able to labour for the benefit of the Company, the welfare of the people, and your own honour and glory, and also to my great joy. I wish all this from a very obedient heart, and recommend myself to your generous favour and innate kindly nature. Martinus Hamerling." A judicious reply was sent on 25 February: "Received his congratulations. Will show him favour according to his conduct and fidelity to the Company." There was a general feeling of relief that the Cape was about to be able to enjoy a period of more stable administration.

There were now two main strands of activity at the Cape. Louis van Assenburgh made a diplomatic start as a wise Governor, although he had the problem of still having Willem Adriaan van der Stel under his feet. The new Governor was anxious not to stir up trouble in what was an awkward situation. On 7 March 1708, the ex-Governor produced a report for his successor in which he criticised the treatment he had received and he stressed how painful his recall to the Fatherland and the disposal of his farm at Vergelegen was to him. He complained that his honour and status had been "most grievously injured" by some freemen of this country by their writing about him in their letters in a "very vile and despicable manner." Protesting that he was a man of honour, he demanded justice for himself and his family before leaving the Cape.

The Commissioner and Governor considered these points but did not feel they had the authority to vary the explicit instructions of the Council of Seventeen. They were acutely aware that the communication from the Seventeen, written in October 1706, had made clear their wish to see the Cape colony restored to peace and trust. Crucial to this end, was the recall of Willem Adriaan van der Stel and his three senior colleagues. Together with his wife and family, the ex-Governor left for Holland without ceremony on the *Oostergeest* at the end of March 1708. He took with him a number of official documents in case an action were to be brought against him in Holland for which he would need to prepare himself. However, no lawsuit was ever raised.

CHAPTER 15

Collapse of the Dutch East India Company

The recall to Holland in 1708 of the disgraced ex-Governor Willem Adriaan van der Stel marked the end of the period of initial growth and consolidation by the Dutch at the Cape. Thereafter, although progress was slow, there was a strong tendency towards an easterly movement beyond the land which had been settled by the first Europeans, within easy reach of Cape Town. This easterly migration was associated with the growing economy of 'trekboer' farming with its widespread pattern of scattered pastoralists, in marked contrast to the previous pattern of sedentary farming and settlement. By 1700, there were about one thousand free burghers at the Cape.

The demanding regulations of the VOC (Dutch East India Company) had been a deterrent rather than an encouragement to settling, and presented a further contrast with Dutch expansion in North America, where growth had been rapid. In 1707 the scheme of free passages from the Netherlands to the Cape was given up. Immigrants were very few and Amsterdam made no effort to add to their number. Even so, over a period of time, a number of migrants to the Cape included Germans anxious to leave central Europe after the devastations of the Thirty Years' War. They made a welcome addition to the Cape population.

By the year 1708, the settlement on the shores of Table Bay had grown unmistakably into the outline of Cape Town, the mother city of South Africa. The two most important assets created by

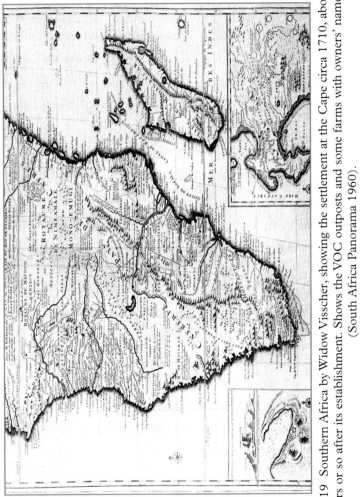

FIGURE 19 Southern Africa by Widow Visscher, showing the settlement at the Cape circa 1710, about fifty years or so after its establishment. Shows the VOC outposts and some farms with owners' names. (South Africa Panorama 1960).

the early VOC settlers were the Company's gardens and the castle. Both symbolized the function of the pioneer: the supply of fresh foodstuffs to the passing fleets and a fortified centre from which the VOC administration was carried out. The servicing of the fleets while anchored in Table Bay was an important and demanding task for the inhabitants. As recorded earlier, the grid plan of the street layout began with the Herrengracht, the main street leading inland from the shore up to the gardens. Smaller streets led off it at right angles to complete the plan, which has remained distinct to this day.

The further development of the Cape community did not run smoothly. Within five years of the departure of Willem Adriaan van der Stel, an outbreak of smallpox in 1713 carried off nearly one quarter of the inhabitants within six weeks. Later in the same year, but not from smallpox, came the death of Louis van Assenburgh, after only five years in office. Further hardships hit in the following year, 1714, when a severe outbreak of animal disease decimated the sheep and cattle population to such an extent that there could be no bidders in 1718 for the annual meat contract. In 1717 further legislation by the VOC put an end to the granting of farmland, partly to reduce the risk of over production of crops, which became a recurrent problem. This regrettable change of policy presented a marked contrast to the farming patterns which the Dutch had developed with such care during the earlier years of their settlement at the Cape.

After 1720, the Council of Seventeen altered its personnel by dropping the merchant representation and replacing it with the nobility and other members of the ruling class. From this time, VOC trade passing through the Cape slackened off with the loss of the exclusive trade in pepper, in the face of greater competition from other European traders, including the English. This trend was not improved by the new structure of the Company. Later in the century, two further outbreaks of smallpox took their toll of the community. In 1755, a homeward bound fleet brought the

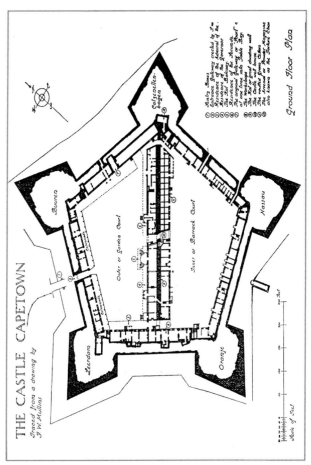

FIGURE 20 Plan of the Castle, Cape Town 1704. From *Historical Atlas of South Africa* by Professor E.A. Walker (courtesy of OUP. Drawn by F.W. Mullins, as adapted in *The Cape of Good Hope 1652–1833* by G.E. Pearse, courtesy of J.L. Van Schaik, Pretoria).

disease from Ceylon and caused the deaths of nine hundred and sixty three Europeans and eleven hundred natives in Cape Town. Twelve years later, in 1767, a Danish ship brought the disease, from which one hundred and seventy nine Europeans, one hundred and forty five natives and two hundred and fifty one slaves died between May and November.

However, these last decades were enhanced by the regime from 1751 to 1771 of Ryk Tulbagh as Governor, who lent stability and wisdom to the deteriorating political situation. The final twenty year period of the Company's rule reflected progressively declining circumstances. The VOC continued to manage the Cape until 1795, when in a spectacular collapse the Dutch East India Company ceased trading under a mountain of debt, and it was finally dissolved in 1799. The British assumed control at the capitulation of Rustenburg. After the colony had changed hands several times, the British took definitive possession of it in 1814 under the Treaty of Paris.

Thus came to an end the Dutch rule at the Cape. The first fifty six years of its regime had left the strongest and most tangible marks of Dutch culture in the area first settled by Europeans. Today, looking at this corner of South Africa, historic Dutch influences are still apparent in a number of ways. In particular, they include Cape Dutch architecture, some culinary traditions and the language, which gradually altered from seventeenth century Dutch to the Afrikaans of the present day.

The harnessing of the Mediterranean-type climate by the three hundred year old Cape wine industry contributed to a broad economic base, using the landscape in an area of great natural beauty. This, together with the pattern of settlement, agriculture, and the shipping prowess of the Dutch East India Company, formed the background to the making of Dutch South Africa.

Bibliography

Axelson, E.V. *South East Africa 1488-1503*, London: Longmans, Green & Co., 1940.

Barnard, Lady A. *South Africa a Century Ago*, ed. W.H. Watkins. London: Smith, Elder & Co., 1908.

Barrow, J. *Travels into the Interior of South Africa*, 2 ed. London: T. Cadell and W. Davies, 1806

Beeckman, D. *A Voyage to Borneo*, London 1718.

Bird, W.W. *State of the Cape of Good Hope in 1822*, London: J. Murray 1823.

Botha, C.G. *Cape of Good Hope Archives. A brief guide for the period 1652-1806*, Cape Town: 1918.

Botha, C.G. *Administration of the Cape 1653-1839.*

Botha, C.G. *Early Development of South Africa.*

Botha, C.G. *Early History of Cape Province.*

Botha, C.G. *The French Refugees at the Cape*, 1919.

Botha, C.G. Collectanea 1st series, Extracts from 'A Voyage to Surat 1689' by J Ovington MA, chaplain to His Majesty, and 'A new Voyage round the World' by Captain William Dampier 1691, Van Riebeeck Society, 1924.

Botha, C.G. *The Public Archives of South Africa, Cape Town*, 1928.

Botha, C.G. *Collected Works* (3 vols.) Struik, 1962.

Boxer, C.R. *The Dutch Seaborne Empire 1600-1800*, 1964.

Boxer, C.R. Tavern of Two Seas, *History Today*, 1964.

Bruce, J. *Annals of the East India Company*, 1968.

Bruijn, J.R. *Dutch-Asiatic Shipping in the Seventeenth and Eighteenth Centuries*, The Hague, 1988.

Burchell, W.J. *Travels in the Interior of Southern Africa*, London: Printed for Longman, Hurst, Rees, Orme and Brown 1822-24 (2 vols.).

Cole, M. *South Africa*, London: 1961 and 1966

Colvin, I. *The Romance of South Africa*, 1909.

Colvin, I. *Cape of Adventure*, 1912.

Cory, G.E. *The Rise of South Africa*, London; Longmans, Green & Co., 1921. (vols. I and II).

Dampier, W. *A new Voyage round the World*, London: 1697.

Dehérain, H. *Le Cap de Bonne-Espérance au XVII Siècle*, Paris: Libraire Hachette, 1909.

De Klerk, W.A. *The Puritans in Africa*, 1975

De Kock, V. *Those in Bondage*, Cape Town: 1950.

De St. Pierre, J.H.B. *A Voyage to the Isle of France, the Isle of Bourbon and the Cape of Good Hope*, London 1800.

Du Plessis, I.D. *The Cape Malays*, Cape Town: Maskew Miller, Limited 1944.

Elphick, R. *Kraal and Castle: Khoikhoi and the founding of White South Africa*, 1977.

Elphick, R and Giliomee, H. eds. *The Shaping of South African Society 1652-1820*, London: Longman, 1979, 2nd edition and 1989.

Fairbridge, D. *Historic Farms of South Africa*, Oxford University Press, Humphrey Milford, 1931.

Fairbridge, D. *Historic Houses of South Africa*, Oxford University Press, Humphrey Milford 1922.

Fairbridge, D. *Lady Anne Barnard at the Cape of Good Hope 1797-1802*, Oxford at the Clarendon Press, 1924.

Fisher, R.B. *The Importance of the Cape of Good Hope as a Colony to Great Britain*, London: 1816.

Fitzroy, V.M. *When the Slave Bell Tolled*, Cape Town: 1970.

Fransen, H. and Cook, M.A. *The Old Buildings of the Cape*, 1900.

Freeman-Grenville, G. *Chronology of African History*, Oxford University Press, 1972.

Goodfellow, D.M. *A Modern Economic History of South Africa*, 1931

Harris, J.A. *A Complete Collection of Voyages and Travels*, 2 ed. London: 1744.

Hellman, E. ed. *Handbook on Race Relations in South Africa*, Oxford University Press, 1949.

Jourdain, J. *The Journal of John Jourdain 1608-1717*, Cambridge. Printed for the Hakluyt Society, 1905.

Juritz, C.F. *A study of the Agricultural Soils of the Cape Colony*, 1909.

Karsten, M.C. *The Old Company's Garden at the Cape*, 1951.

Kendall, F.K. *The Restoration of Groot Constantia*, Cape Town: Juta & Co. Ltd., 1926.

Kench, J. *Cape Dutch Homesteads*, 1981.

Kolbe, P. *Caput Bonae Spei Hodiernum*, Nuremburg: 1719.

Kwamena-Poh, M. *African History in the Making*, Longmans, 1982.

Lamar, H and Thompson, L. *The frontiers in History: North America and South Africa Compared*, 1981.

Leguat, F. *A new Voyage to the East Indies*, London:1708.

Leibbrandt, H.C.V. *Rambles through the Archives of the Cape of Good Hope 1688-1700.*

Leibbrandt, H.C.V. *Précis of the Archives of the Cape of Good Hope. Containing Letters Received and Letters Despatched 1695-1708*, 3 vols. Cape Town: W.A. Richards & Sons, 1896-1900.

Leipoldt, C.G.L. *Biography of Jan van Riebeeck*, Longmans, 1936.

Leipoldt, C.F.L. *Three Hundred Years of Cape Wine*, 1952

Leppan, H.D. and Bosmer, G.J. *Field Crops in South Africa*, Royal Geographic Society.

Macmillan, W.M. *Bantu, Boer and Briton*, Oxford University Press, revised ed., 1963 (original 1928)

Marais, J.S. *The Cape Coloured People 1652-1937*, Longmans, 1939.

Mayer, P. *Townsmen and Tribesmen*, 1961.

Mentzel, O.F. *A Complete and Authentic Geographical and Topographical Description of the Cape of Good Hope, Glogau 1785.* Cape Town: Van Riebeeck Society, (vol. 4), 1921.

Moodie, D. *The Records of the Cape*, 1960.

Moodie, D. *Specimens of the Authentic Records of the Cape.*

Mossop, E.E. *Old Cape Highways.*

Nathan, M. *The Huguenots in South Africa*, South Africa Central News Agency, 1939.

Ovington, J. A *Voyage to Surat*, London: 1696.

Percival, R. *An Account to the Cape of Good Hope*, London. 1804.

Pearse, G.E. *The Cape of Good Hope 1652-1833*, J.L Van Shaik Ltd., Pretoria: 1956.

Pollock, N.C. *Africa*, University of London Press, 1968.

Poole, R.L. *A History of the Huguenots and the Dispersion*, 1880.

Raven-Hart, R. *Cape of Good Hope 1652-1702, the first fifty years of Dutch colonisation as seen by Callers*, 2 vols. Cape Town: A.A. Balkema, 1971.

Ross, R. *Cape of Torments: Slavery and Resistance in South Africa*, Routledge, 1983.

Shapera, I. *The early Cape Hottentots*, ed.1933.

Sleigh, D. *The world of the Dutch East India Company*, Cape Town, Tafelberg, 1980

Spilhaus, M.W. *The First South Africans*, 1949.

Spilhaus, M.W. *Indigenous Trees of the Cape Peninsula*, 1950

Spilhaus, M.W. *South Africa in the Making 1652-1805*, 1966.

Spilhaus, M.W. *Company's Men*, 1973.

Tachard, G. *Voyage de Siam des Pères Jésuites*, Paris: 1686.

Theal, G.M. *Chronicles of the Cape Commanders,* Cape Town: W.A. Richards & Sons, 1882.

Theal, G.M. *History and Ethnography of South Africa before 1795* (2 vols.) London: 1909.

Theal, G.M. *Willem Adriaan van der Stel and other historical sketches,* Cape Town: 1913.

Theal, G.M. *Abstract of the Debates and Resolutions of the Council of Policy, 1651-1687.*

Trotter, A.F. *Old Colonial Houses of the Cape of Good Hope,* London: B.T. Batsford 1900.

Trotter, A.F. *Old Cape Colony.* London, Selwyn and Blount Ltd. 1903.

Troup, F. *South Africa – a historical introduction.* London 1872.

Van Riebeeck, J. *Journal of Jan van Riebeeck* (3 vols.) Van Riebeeck Society, 1952.

Viney, G and Proust, A. *Colonial Houses of South Africa circa 1985.*

Walker, E.A. *A History of South Africa,* London: Longmans, Green & Co. Ltd., 1928.

Walker, E.A. *Historical Atlas of South Africa,* Oxford University Press.

Wickins, P. *An Economic History of Africa,* 1981.

Worden, N.,Van Heyningen, E., Beckford-Smith, V. *Cape Town: The Making of a City,* Cape Town, David Philip, 1998.

Wyatt Tilby, A. *The English People Overseas, South Africa 1486-1912,* (vol.vii), 1914.